Crashed

ALSO BY MELINDA FERGUSON

Smacked
Hooked
The Kelly Khumalo Story
Oscar: An Accident Waiting to Happen

PUBLISHED BY MFBOOKS JOBURG

The Goddess Bootcamp
The Kelly Khumalo Story
Boy
Drug Muled
Dwelmslagoffer
Dystopia
A Renegade Called Simphiwe
Marrying Black Girls for Guys Who Aren't Black
Catastrophe: Oy Vey, My Child is Gay
Oscar: An Accident Waiting to Happen
Bollywood Blonde
Rough Diamond
When Loving him Hurts
Rape: A South African Nightmare

Crashed

Melinda Ferguson

WHAT THEY SAID ABOUT SMACKED:

"A truly courageous hero, you've got to hear this woman's story."
– JOHN ROBBIE, RADIO 702

"It's real and shocking. It's Trainspotting meets Hillbrow. It's a story you won't soon forget and a lesson you never should."
– COSMOPOLITAN

"This is a story of tremendous courage that plunges into the alleys, veins and valleys of a drug addict, emerging victorious."
– NKHENSANI MANGANYI NKOSI, STONED CHERRIE

"A remarkable solo journey, plunging to hell and beyond and then soaring to redemption and life."
– DARRYL ACCONE

"An inspiration. Made me cry."
– PATRICK HOLFORD, THE OPTIMUM NUTRITION BIBLE

"A gritty tale that will shove itself right up into your perfect little world and scream, 'Hello, I am addiction.' The question is do you want to face it?"
– KELLY ANSARA, IT'S A BOOK THING BLOG

"Smacked, it's one hell of a ride."
– MICHELLE McGRANE, LITNET

To Mat

First published by MFBooks Joburg, an imprint of
Jacana Media (Pty) Ltd, in 2015

10 Orange Street
Sunnyside
Auckland Park 2092
South Africa
+2711 628 3200
www.jacana.co.za

ISBN 978-1-920601-60-7

Cover design by publicide
Set in Sabon 11/15pt
Printed and bound by ABC Press, Cape Town
Job no. 002594

Also available as an e-book:
d-PDF ISBN 978-1-920601-61-4
ePUB ISBN 978-1-920601-62-1
mobi file ISBN 978-1-920601-63-8

See a complete list of Jacana titles at www.jacana.co.za

Contents

Acknowledgments

To my darling sons James and Daniel who have lived through five books with me and the year of The Crash, and still love me. I adore you to the end of the universe and beyond.

Thank you my dear friends Val, Martine, Kate, Peta, Megan, Pumla and Daryl as well as my brother, Neil and sister, Joanne – for always seeing me through with love.

To my ex-colleagues Zama, Zinhle, Lerato, Mokgadi, Farrah, Refilwe, Thami – we went through some rough seas but sunshine days are upon us. You are always in my heart.

Kaya FM, Sagie Moodley and The Joy Ride, thank you for revving right by my side.

To all those in the motoring industry who gave me their much-needed love and support: Lesley Sutton, Denis Droppa, Ferrari at Viglietti Motors, Chanelle Zackey, Liana Reiners, Christo Valentyn, Aurelia Mbokazi, Mabuyane Kekane, Toni Herbst, Glen Hill, Rella Bernades, James Siddell, Tracey de Late, Minesh Bhagaloo, Megan McDonald, Shirle Greig, Andile Dlamini, Stuart Johnston, Joeline Dabrowski, Edward Makwana, Clynton Yon, Kerrie Roodt, Lindsey Pieterse, Adell de Vos, Tasneem Lorgat and anyone else I may have overlooked – thank you.

Bridget Impey and Maggie Davey – thank you for believing in me as a publisher and writer. I still sometimes pinch myself when

I see my imprint logo on a book cover. And to Kerrie, Shay, Meg, Janine and Asanda and all the other great staff at Jacana – thanks.

Thanks Sean Fraser for being a great editor – your eye was always on target.

Owen Blumberg, my amazing attorney who got me out of some very, very hectic places. Thank you thank you thank you.

Thank you to Lili and Nic for opening up your beautiful hearts to me.

Now for the Love of my Life, Mat. You have walked through this book, held my hand and my heart and on all the days I've misbehaved and tantrumed, been precious and stupidly "artistic" – you have been right at my side, word for word, page by page.

When I met you Nick Cave's "Are you the one I've been waiting for?" kept playing wherever I went. I know for sure that each day that I wake up with you, that the answer is, yes.

That I feed the hungry, forgive an insult, and love my enemy ... all these are undoubtedly great virtues ... But what if I should discover ... that the poorest of beggars, the most impudent of offenders are within me, and that I stand in need of the alms of my own kindness – that I myself am the enemy who must be loved – what then?
– CG JUNG, MEMORIES, DREAMS, REFLECTIONS

CHAPTER 1

Crashed

I suppose my own internal crash – spectacular as it was – all started with a little red car. The Ferrari.

Spring Day, 1 September 2013, was my 14-year birthday clean and sober and this was the year I had planned to celebrate it like never before. That night I'd given a talk at a Narcotics Anonymous Parkhurst recovery meeting, during which I could hardly contain my exuberance when I told the group that, within a few hours, I would be collecting one of the biggest gifts I could ever have imagined receiving in recovery. A rare R3.2-million four-seater Ferrari California to review for the day.

I hadn't actually believed Ferrari would honour my request to take out their Cali, but they had – with a gracious smile, in fact. Higher-power stuff, I grinned to myself. As a motoring journalist, I was blessed to drive hot new wheels on a weekly basis, but the Ferrari was in another league all together.

This was a convertible GT, packing 338kW of V8 power, and as I signed the indemnity forms at the dealership the following morning, it felt like a pure poetic universal blessing. What a reward for staying on my journey of recovery for a whole 14 years; what better way to pat myself on the back – give that girl a round of Bell's, figuratively speaking of course – than by being handed the keys of a R3.2-bar gleaming red Italian super car in

1

which to cruise the streets of my hometown? Even if it was only for a day.

I didn't read much on the forms I signed; I was on far too much of a buzz. I half heard that the car was insured, but in the event of an accident I would be liable for 10 per cent excess. No sweat, baby. But I did manage to pay attention when the guy told me to have the vehicle back by 4 pm, at which point the insurance would cease. He also warned me not to activate Launch Control, which would normally be used for track driving, as insurance wouldn't pay in the unlikely event of a crash. I smiled. For a moment I felt like I was on an aeroplane listening to the prerequisite emergency safety instructions. Crash landing. I grinned and nodded in agreement to everything he was babbling on about as he showed me how to switch her on and off and how to adjust the seats.

It was just after 9 am when, roof down, long hair gleaming in GHD glory – I had had it done the previous day to complete my über-cool super-car look – I drove out of the dealership on William Nicol Drive, Johannesburg. I had never experienced anything quite like this. Zero to a hundred in 3.5 seconds, with a growl that swallowed the tar, I felt like the Queen of Wheels, on top of the world.

As I pulled up at The Magazine's Sandton office there was a flurry as friends and staff swarmed round in a frenzy to take photos and touch the Italian beauty in her glorious red aluminium flesh.

I stood back like a proud pet owner, a parent who had just birthed the Saviour, a Buddha babe. The new Dalai Lama. It felt like my entire life had been leading to this moment. Fuck *The Monk Who Sold His Ferrari* – mine would be bigger. I could see the title of my next bestselling book: *From Homeless Farm to Ferrari* ... I had arrived.

I turned the key in the ignition of the Cali and gave her a little rev. The crowd roared in approval. I then parked her on the rooftop parking, where I could keep an eye on her, my beloved machine, from my desk. Man, was I just loving this, revelling in the moment.

Throughout the day, the compact sports car took up a lot more time and energy than I had bargained for. Just as I would seat myself behind my desk and try to get the day's work started, someone would ask for a ride and, before I knew it, four of us would be squeezed into the car and I'd be coasting around Sandton, ogled by every motorist and pedestrian who crossed our path.

By the time I dropped my son and his cousin at home – I'd picked them up at school around lunchtime to give them the coolest experience of their lives – I was well and truly exhausted. At this point, all I really wanted to do was chill, but the clock was ticking toward the agreed return time and, as I stood up from my desk to make that final journey back to the dealership, three of my colleagues who had not yet savoured Cali magic begged me for one last ride. If I had done what I had felt like doing at this point, I would have said no. I was tired and worried about getting the car back by 4 pm. It was already 3:20 pm. What if there was an unexpected hold-up, a robot down, a power failure on Sandton Drive, as there so often was at this time these days? I needed to leave. Now.

But instead of saying no, I sighed inwardly, smiled and agreed for the girls to accompany me.

"People pleaser," I snarled to myself.

Some of the top talent at The Mag, the Food Ed, the Deputy Ed, the Copy Ed and I made our way to the rooftop parking. Before we left we took a group selfie and posted it on Instagram. Then I pumped up the jam and we headed out of the parking lot, some dope Lil Wayne blaring from the speakers. It felt like we were cruising Miami. By the time "No Scrubs" kicked into gear, the world was ours for the taking, all 338 kilowatts of power bursting to life.

This little Italian bitch of a ride needed very little coaxing. With her quick throttle response, within nanoseconds of pressing my foot on the edge of the accelerator she was begging for more in a hysterical cadenza of dizzying revs. She could have pushed Primal Scream off the charts.

Instead of heading into rush-hour traffic, I decided to rather err on the side of safety and work my way along the back routes, through Benmore, a small-business-type residential suburb, just in case the main route was jammed up. It was 3:25 pm, plenty of time to travel the 7-kilometre journey back to Cali's palace on William Nicol.

Parked in neutral at the red light, crossing into Benmore, I couldn't help but appreciate the great ironies in my life. Perched behind the tiny leather-bound steering wheel of this mega-million super car, images of what I once was exactly 14 years ago flashed before me: homeless, abandoned, addicted, trapped on a beggars' farm in the middle of nowhere, on the bones of my then drug-depleted, malnutritioned skinny 48-kilogram white ass, hacking, coughing, lungs bleeding, a shell of a human, begging for oblivion, at the doorway of death.

For fuck's sake, I grinned to myself, how amazing was life? How much could one person's entire existence change? Forget 360 degrees – mine was a 720-degree double revolution. I mean, I was the girl who was never going to drive. "The more you drive the less intelligent you are" – I had held onto that mantra for many years, the one from Alex Cox's *Repo Man*, while I proceeded to get loaded, sprawled out on the back seat of other people's cars as they ferried my usually inebriated self from A to B, backwards and forwards.

And now this.

I revved a little and checked my reflection in the rear-view mirror from behind D&G shades I'd bought for a fortune in the Roppongi district while attending the Tokyo Motor Show a few years earlier. God, I was a lucky bitch, I smirked. *The Cat that Got the Cali*. Another good chapter title for the book I was itching to write.

On 11th Avenue, a long single-lane street that stretched almost all the way to connect with William Nicol, we found ourselves stuck behind a large delivery truck travelling at a snail's pace. Fucking, hello? We were now forced to crawl at 20 kilometres per hour in a car that could screech to 100 kilometres in less than four seconds.

I checked for oncoming traffic. Nothing for as far as I could see – the long road to the right completely clear. Here was my chance. I could rev her up, overtake this slow boat and get a bit of open tar to show my girls what this beauty could do. It seemed like the simplest thing in the world. I touched the right pedal, and she growled with impending pleasure. I began my move.

And then, just as I sailed past the truck to nip back in and take my space on the left – I could not have been moving faster than 50 – I saw it. It would be an image that would continue to haunt me.

A flash of red.

An almighty meeting of metal on metal, a thunderous crash from Thor's mansion in the sky and then a blur: a fast spin into a spectacular vortex, round and round into a cyclone of uncontrolled motion, swallowed up into a ravenous 12-metre wave of timelessness, a free-spinning roll of air. There was no sound, just the deathly choir of angels waiting to receive us.

On and on we spun. We seemed to whirl forever. And then suddenly it all slowed down … time distorted like a 45 single playing on 33.

And then I felt it, the White Light. It came in from above, descended and encased us.

Like a monster shadow, it wrapped itself around me, around my everything. It took control like a lioness holds her litter, swirled around the spinning red and brought it to its knees. Everything stopped for the very longest time. It grew quieter, quieter than the dead end of time. The silence was impenetrable. Nothing moved. Then I breathed for the first time. I was alive.

And then the screaming began.

"My baby! My baby!" I heard a woman wailing.

Slowly, catatonic, I opened the driver's door. The red car lay sprawled in jagged fragments across the tar, like a toy that had been pummelled by a hammer, a mashed-up sardine can, road kill festering in the sun.

Across from me, on the other side of the road, a seven-seat Pajero stood rammed up on the pavement, left side smashed. The traffic light lay on the pavement, dismembered, the amber light still flashing. I moved across the road, slow like a donkey slouching to Bethlehem in Yeats's "The Second Coming". The driver of the Pajero was holding her baby. They were both alive. No blood.

The vultures were gathering fast. Phones whipped out, cameras clicking. Ambulance sirens screeched in. The appearance of tow-truck scavengers – six of them – was almost immediate. Within minutes, a sicko blogger who follows crashes posted images of the crushed red metal disaster on his website.

News of the crash spread like an oil spill on social media. Twitter and Facebook were jam-packed with threads of dreck. Malicious jibes and comments of glee from fellow motoring journos were some of the worst.

Thankfully, I refused to engage with any of the debased cruelty that erupted straight after the crash. In that dark post-crash depression I may very well have topped myself if I had.

The following morning Gareth Cliff gloated about it for ten minutes on 5FM's breakfast show. By Sunday the newspapers were running page-three stories: "Bestselling author writes off rare R3.2 million Ferrari."

Months later, when I am brave enough to look, I am shocked at how heartless humanity can really be. But the defamatory comments that probably hurt most were those around my sobriety and assumptions that I had relapsed on a crazy binge of crack and alcohol. Jokes about women drivers were par for the course. Of course.

Back at the accident scene, spaced out in shock, I numbly turned to check on my three passengers … Everyone was alive but stumbling around like zombies. The Food Ed had blood running from above her eye and, for a second, I thought she had lost her eye. The Copy Ed kept on repeating, "My phone, my phone." Her BlackBerry lay crushed on the tar next to my mutilated D&Gs. The Deputy Ed walked in circles, shaken, eyes glazed over.

Then some vague thread of logic kicked in. I looked at the time on my phone, which had somehow remained unscathed in the pocket of my leather jacket. It was 3:45 pm. Insurance. A bolt of panic shot through me. I needed to phone the car dealer to alert the insurance before 4 pm. That was the agreement.

Somehow I found the strength to dial the number.

"Hello? Hello, Tracey?"

A woman's voice answered.

"Hello, hello? Can you hear me? Something terrible's happened. An accident. You have to come quickly – now. Benmore 11th ... You'll see it – there are people everywhere."

"I'm sure it's fine. Just stay calm – we're on our way ..." the voice on the other end of the line said.

"No, you don't understand ... It's not fine. It's really, really fucked. It's not fine ... not fine at all."

I dropped the call. I wanted to be sick. Where was my pink leather handbag?

JG Ballard, the British author, once described a car crash as the most dramatic event we are likely to experience in our entire lives – "apart from our own deaths".

It was an accident that changed me forever.

CHAPTER 2

Hotel Hospital

I booked myself into a rehab clinic exactly six months later. I hadn't relapsed. In fact, I was now 14 and a half years clean and sober ... That's 5 182 Just-for-Today days and a fuck load of 24 hours. About 124 000-plus. The Hotel Hospital, with its swaying palm trees and sparkling fountain, also catered for Depression/ Anxiety, Burnout, Psychosis, Eating Disorders, Post-Traumatic Stress Disorder and Schizophrenia. I qualified for at least three.

I hadn't relapsed on drugs or booze. Yet.

But I had been howling for weeks, salt mines of sorrow.

I wondered if a person could die from crying.

My dehydrated eyes were now barren pits as I passed through the boom of the upmarket joint and parked the car in Visitors. It was an Audi, I think. The S3 S-Tronic: 2-litre model. DSG gearbox. Zero to 1000 kilometres in five seconds. I'd been re-viewing it that week. Actually, it could have been a Mito. Alfa. Jesus, I was losing it. It had been happening more and more. Forgetting things. I guess the fact that I was still getting cars to test drive and review, after the monumental metal disaster, was something of a miracle.

Everything had become a blur since The Crash.

An accident can cause chaos. And mine was spectacular. Huge bills. No sleep. Police statements. Lawyers. PTSD. Internal hearings at work. Crazy food behaviour. Nervous burnout. All those twenty-first-century maladies.

If I were an animal I would have been tearing fur from my coat. Big chunks. If I'd been a cutter my skin would have been in shreds.

The Crash was one of a number of reasons I found myself waking up that April Tuesday morning, packing two suitcases and driving north into rush hour, bleary from my usual less than three hours of mind-racing-interrupted sleep. And even though it had happened six months earlier, the experts would later concur that The Crash was probably the primary underlying reason for my own, internal crash. So let's keep it top of mind and, for the record, call it Reason 1.

On the Hotel Hospital website there were clear instructions on what to bring: *only pack appropriate casual, comfortable clothing.* I brought along a lot of shoes. A whole suitcase full, in fact. Kenneth Coles, Aldos, Steve Maddens and Guess. Shoes always made me feel strangely elevated; the more inappropriate the better.

The *What to Bring* also said: No sharp objects allowed. I decided to leave my Swiss Army knife in the cubbyhole of the car.

The surrounding palm trees and ochre clay fountain at the entrance made me feel like I was on a movie set in an apocalyptic future-fucked Miami; there was a heavy tinge of toxic green in the murky water. All that was missing were the fish. Perhaps they'd died. Somehow the forlorn pond reminded me of the goldfish I kept replacing when my two sons were little. I had never managed to keep their gold-finned pets alive. I wondered if they resented me for this now that they were teenagers.

My multiple years of Clean and Serene NA key rings jangled as I walked into reception. I had a bunch of them. What a fucking irony. *Clean and sober*, in gold-embossed lettering. Whoever said that with sobriety came serenity must have been smoking something – something potent. I had long since lost my serenity. Right now it felt like I was holding on to my clean time like the sole survivor in a zombie holocaust, as though my eyes had been pecked out of my skull. That can happen when the man you love, who you think you'll live with for the rest of your life, betrays you.

But the more immediate catalyst, what had literally sent me over the edge, was a far more recent occurrence. For purposes of clarity, this one will be Reason 2: My Broken Heart.

A lion hates to be double-crossed. And I, being a Leo, felt as if I had been brutalised, my heart shredded into slivers.

The Hotel Hospital had once been a bar-cum-nightclub, and the architecture – high ceilings, ballrooms, chandeliers, mirrored pillars, brown wood panelling – managed to give it an other-worldly feel. I almost expected a ghost waiter in a Stetson and tailcoat to offer me a drink.

I'd decided to leave my bags and a mountain of belongings in the Audi – just in case I changed my mind. I always brought half my life with me whenever there was a possibility that I may have to stay overnight. This probably stems from when I had been homeless back in 1999. Post my drug apocalypse. When I landed on that homeless farm up in the Magaliesberg just off the R512 – after I'd smoked up my entire life in exchange for the high you get from a hit of crack or a lungful of amnesia, from chasing the dragon, from a deep pull of smack.

With no more than a single plastic bag containing three dresses – donated by some God-fearing Christian do-gooder, along with a coffee-stained Bible – I had experienced what it felt to lose everything and own nothing. To become dependent on the kindness of strangers like a fallen woman in a Tennessee Williams play.

At night , in a mouldy-ceilinged room on the farm, as I searched for sleep, I had been forced to confront my "things we lost in the fire" feelings. My demons almost killed me. To simply end it all seemed inevitable. What else was there to do with a life that had simply ceased to be worth waking up for?

But I didn't. I didn't pull the trigger, take the pills, shoot up the veins, snuff the breath, cut the blood supply. Instead I managed to stumble forward, one minute, one hour, one day at a time and, miraculously, I made it across the bridge of death where black crows caw and vultures bicker over bones.

Later, when sanity returned, I would take great solace from the line in Chuck Palahniuk's *Fight Club* that says that it's only after you lose everything that you are free to do anything.

But that Great Disaster That Was Once My Sad Pathetic Life had happened such a very long time ago. I thought I was cured, that I was better, that those lesions that life had left, deep etched into me, would have prevented me from ever falling down another catastrophic black hole. How could all this be happening again?

I was, however, well on the way to discovering a sad truth about human behaviour: that no matter how hard the fall, the mind often has a cunning way of anaesthetising the lessons we should learn from Pain.

And even though my Samsonite and Thule suitcases were now filled with designer gear – Karen Millen, Thomas Pink, Dolce & Gabbana; even though my life had transformed three billion degrees from the hacking-coughing-junkie-ho I had once been, even though, even though, even though ... the truth was that the same terrible sense of an imminent implosion had taken me right back to that place of Everything Is Over.

And here, staring at these haunting surroundings, it felt like nothing had changed, the picture had remained much the same – the only real differences were the palm trees and the manor-house façade, as opposed to the rubble and dilapidation of that place called Homeless.

I stared at the glass-and-walnut doors leading into the Hotel Hospital; there was still time to turn back. I had filled in no forms. Made no promises. Signed no papers.

I thought about one of my favourite The Clash songs, "Should I stay or should I go?" and how quickly days turn from gold to black.

Was I about to lose it in a loony bin? Become Alice in Chains? Lucy in the sky with diamonds? The terror mounted. Would the long and winding road lead me back, homeless again?

CHAPTER 3

Admissions

I stared into nothing as I waited on the couch for the woman from Admissions. Fuck, what was her name? I'd been forgetting the most mundane things lately, and it was getting worse and worse. I knew she had told me. Yesterday. When I'd desperately called her, talking in rising hysterical tones from my desk in the open-plan office at The Magazine.

Jeanie ... Janie ... Jinny? If I made my way through the letters in the alphabet, maybe I'd get it eventually. Sometimes that worked. Genie. That was it! Similar name to that of my oldest sister. My somewhat estranged sibling. It had taken years to rebuild the broken bridges and mayhem caused by *Smacked,* my tell-all drug memoir. The one that had desecrated me, my family and its belief systems.

Scorched and Burned.

I guess, in writing my story, I had used similar tactics to that adopted by Stalin against the Nazis in World War II. My own Scorched Earth policy – a military strategy that involves destroying, often burning, anything that might be useful to the enemy while advancing through or withdrawing from an area. Somehow, owning your own truth, your own disaster, gives you a little more power than if others own your truth. My book was pretty hardcore stuff, not easily forgotten or forgiven. But somehow of great benefit – and despite the path of destruction it may have left in its wake – to the perpetrator; in my case, to me, the writer. In the case of my family, for many years, it created instant and long-term alienation.

In fact, despite a number of attempts at apology, it took a long time before any real reconciliation with my sister ever took place. These days we were forced to keep a geographical distance. She lived in the north. In Sweden, to be precise. In the ice. I preferred the south. It was warmer.

It takes a lot to say sorry, but perhaps it takes even more to forgive.

She had sounded sweet on the phone, this Hotel Hospital Genie woman. Motherly, even. Not like my stern Germanic mother. Fuck. Suddenly I missed her. It happened sometimes, leaping out of nowhere; a longing for my mom would sweep in, at a traffic light, in a queue. Quite uninvited, it would arrive like a black crow and nestle in my neck and drag out my tears.

She'd been buried almost a decade. Cremated, actually. Even though our mother was never one who would go along with any of those Eastern beliefs, my sister had insisted that she be burned. With death, our mom had lost her right to argue.

At the end all we had was a little box of ashes. I don't think my mother would have approved.

Truth be told, I hadn't really liked her. Loved her – sure, she was my only parent – but liked? No, not very much at all when she'd been alive.

But here, about to check into this strange clinic that looked like a hotel, I felt my aloneness, my umbilical cordless-ness so acutely that the ache all but ripped right into the place where they had once cut and tied the feeding line at birth. I had never felt further away from a place called home, even when I had been homeless. A little speck spinning in some faraway black hole. Lost out there in the horizonless *Star Trek* of a place they call space.

The feeling of free falling might have had something to do with the fact that I had hardly told a soul I was heading here. Not even my brother. The one person I did tell, however, was my publisher at The Magazine. Concerned by my recent downward spiral, I think she was relieved to see me go off to get help.

It must have been hard not to notice that I had been growing progressively more fucked up at work since The Crash. Drowning daily in a symphony of wayward sobs. Sometimes hourly. Over the past six months, tears had spread like the slime of nuclear waste; I had shed so many that they had all but eaten through the thread-bare office carpet that coated the floor beneath my swivel chair.

But yesterday was by far the worst. Even before I got in to work, the tears had already taken me hostage. Although who could blame me really? After what happened on The Weekend.

By the time the two young journos I managed got to the office, I was crouched on the floor. Half kneeling, and rocking like a crazy daisy. Awkwardly, they tried to comfort me, but as I looked up helplessly at them, I noticed the "What the fuck are we to do with the boss?" fear in their eyes. That really made me howl. I didn't care that by this stage 30-or-so people, including the entire Sales and Marketing team and writers from two other magazines, were peering over from their desks. I felt no shame. The ability to control myself had long since left as I leopard crawled back to my station.

It was at that point that I Googled the clinic. A white mansion-like building filled the screen. It looked like airbrushed heaven, or at the very least, like a five-star hotel. Sounds of tranquillity accompanied the visuals. They may have mixed in a few early-morning bird calls, which faded into a stream bubbling over smooth pebbles … Contact numbers appeared on the top left of the screen. The toll free 086 number was discreet.

So I had made the call.

Now, perched on the edge of the leather couch in reception, I prayed no one I knew would see me. What if someone from Narcotics Anonymous had booked in? Or perhaps someone I knew was working as a counsellor here? I knew a few addicts who had done that. Become counsellors when they got clean. They had usually fucked up their lives so badly – lying, stealing, running from the cops and SARS – that they were mostly unemployable, so had little choice but to open rehabs. Establish secondary care, halfway establishments. Sober houses.

To give nobility to the cause, someone would inevitably quote Step 12 of the programme: "Help the addict who still suffers." But in some instances it looked, to me, a lot like the blind leading the blind, and over time I had grown increasingly suspicious that many of those who established these "recovery" facilities had ulterior motives: ego and money. The two were intertwined. In fact, some of them were actually more wasted in the head than the addicts they were taking large amounts of money from to "help". And then of course there were the Svengalis who used their sexual magnetism to prey on newly clean addicts, who invariably fell to pieces after they'd been fucked with and often went back "out there" to use again. A lot came close to dying, some even did.

Sitting in reception, I suddenly saw the insanity of my train of thought. Here I was, at this pathetically low juncture in my life, and I was taking the world's inventory. That's what we addicts often do; the more fucked up we feel inside, the easier it is to glare at the world and shoot scud missiles at anything that moves.

At this inglorious point of my existence I'd slid right down to Step 1, blubbering my way back to "I came to believe that my life was unmanageable". Lately I had really been struggling to admit that there was a power greater than me that could restore my sanity.

I hadn't been to a meeting in months. It felt like the more fucked up I was getting, the more I was struggling to get into the circle of NA again. I knew this was a bad place for me to be. In fact, the last time I had actually really shared at a meeting was on 1 September 2013. My 14-year clean birthday. The Crash had happened on 2 September.

Right now, as I peeped from behind my blinkers and confronted the state of my being, I was terrified. How could it all have gone so horribly wrong?

* * *

15

"Hey, Mel! What are you doing here. Have you come to share?"

Fuckfuckityfuck. Just what I'd dreaded. I recognised the voice immediately. "My name is Jax – I'm an addict" – an older guy I'd met in Yeoville back in the nineties. Before I'd started smoking heroin and crack. Jax, who had once walked up and down Rocky Street, bare-footed and unkempt, selling wind chimes to feed his intravenous smack habit. Although I had noticed back then how swollen and purple his sandalled feet always looked, I had been innocent enough to be entirely unaware of the ravages that heroin leaves behind.

Today expensive trainers covered those toes.

He had always been cool to me, especially in those early days when I stumbled into the rooms of recovery, fresh off the streets of Hillbrow, crack-skittish, skinny and coughing like a hag. He'd welcomed me.

He had been almost two years clean by the time we had reconnected at one of my first NA meetings back in 1999. Two whole fucking years. That had seemed like an impossibility for me back then. Stringing 24 hours together felt like Everest. Never mind a full 365 days x 2 = 730 fucking days. No fucking way could I even begin to grasp that.

Clean-shaven, smiling and employed, I'd barely recognised him. Later I would become tremendously inspired by the transformation I saw in him.

At six weeks clean and sober, I think I'd stuck my hands down his pants, somewhere in the Karoo, on the way to a convention in Cape Town. Why couldn't I remember details? Oh fuck, had I given him a blowjob? The once-murky memory suddenly started shifting sharply into focus. And now, here in reception at the Hotel Hospital, I found myself staring blankly at him. The image of me going down on him wouldn't let up. He had this weird smile on his face. Like he remembered too.

But what the hell was he doing here? Oh fuck. Of course, now I remembered – he worked here.

He was one of the few addicts-turned-counsellors who did know what he was doing. There was no way I could get away, spirit myself away and out of this one.

"Burnout, no sleep, my nine-year relationship's over. And I crashed a car. I haven't relapsed – it's just that I'm fucked. Can't stop crying," I muttered, before a deep hiccup released a torrent of sobs. Jesus! Now I dissolved into another flood of tears. No hiding, no pretences. Fuck. Why did I always have to blurt it all out like some errant hosepipe. Now it was probably going to get out, slide away like a sick snake of rumour: "You hear? She's relapsed … Oh, my word, after 14 years! Can you believe it?" Those toxic little addicts always feasting and burping like maggots on chaos to make themselves feel better.

"I haven't relapsed …" I said it again, before finally petering out. A pathetic bleat. As though relapsing was some terrible, seeping venereal disease.

"That's cool. Don't worry," he awkwardly tried to comfort me. "I won't say anything. I work here – anonymity and all, you know. Part of the job. Everyone's got burnout. It's a New Millennium thing. Sometimes I wish I could book in myself. You're doing the right thing." And then, as he moved away, he grinned. "Welcome to The Clinic."

His attempts at comforting me, consoling me, left no impression. I was too way gone for sweet talk. Maybe I had relapsed? I obsessed. Maybe I had gone swinging like a pendulum backwards into that never-ending cycle of need: use-greed-use-need-greed-use.

Relationship addiction. Work addiction. Crazy thought addiction. Facebook. Instagram … And then this fucking thing with food. And actually, while I was at it, probably sex addiction too.

"You're in relapse mode," my longtime therapist, Dr ParaFreud, with little round shrink glasses, whom I hadn't spoken to in three years, had told me when I called him on his cellphone that Sunday – family time, out of office – without even wondering whether I was being inappropriate. "Unbounderised," he would have called it.

"As much as you are in some type of crisis, don't you think you are being a little over dramatic, Melinda? I don't think you actually need to book into a *treatment* centre. You're successful, you've written books, published books. You have your life

17

together. I think you're just going through a hard time. You just need to realign things, put new boundaries in place. Keep going to therapy."

And on some level he was right. Maybe I was being extreme. I'd always been a bit of a drama queen – I'd been told that often enough. Another thing to throw into the Addiction closet, Addicted to Drama. I had even got a degree in it from UCT. "Why you'd need to study it – Drama – I'll never know," my mother had often said. "Your whole life's an act. You are one big drama."

My mother's cruelty, her sharp, uncensored tongue, had the power to hurtle me into alleyways of self-doubt. I remember those deflated moments well. The way her words cut me up like soggy stir-fry.

Genie arrived with the forms. She informed me medical aid had approved the "hospitalisation". Fuck. Hospitalisation at Hotel Hospital. That was serious. Plus, I've always been suspicious of the use of too much alliteration ...

Were they going to put me on a drip, the dreaded intravenous approach? Hook me up with nasty needles?

I signed on the dotted line.

"I'm only staying for seven days," I snarled.

She smiled and nodded.

She instructed me to wait on the couch to be taken up to the nurses' station. Now there was no going back, no reversing.

My mind once again hurtled back to what Dr ParaFreud had advised me. Sure, he may have been right about the outwardly successful part. For more than a decade I had been more than holding it together: author of two bestselling books on addiction. The third on township pop princess Kelly Khumalo, which had sold rather well. I had just finished my fourth – on that stump-legged athlete – which was waiting in the wings to be published. An award-winning magazine writer turned publisher. On the outside, it all looked fabulous ... Here I was, a well-paid speaker at functions touted on my agent's website as a *Famous Speaker* under the category of *Inspirational*. Paid thousands to talk for less than an hour on my journey to hell and back.

"Manifest your lives," I'd tell the audience. "Inspiring", "strong", "courageous" are what other people called me.

I had money in the bank. Fifty pairs of shoes in my closet. I even had a Kate Unger dress for meetings to impress. I did all my banking online with a zooty app on my iPad Air. I had almost paid off my bond. I had medical aid, retirement funds and life insurance. I had Voyager miles, eBucks and Vitality points. I could even choose which lounge I wanted to chill in when I was travelling by air, for fuck's sake.

But since when did a person's outsides become a barometer for the catastrophes we carry inside? The voice inside sneered.

And why, you might ask, in the light of all I had achieved and owned, was I falling about on the floor in floods of tears? Like my epiglottis was about to throttle me? As desperately as I wanted to believe Dr ParaFreud, I knew that this time he was wrong. *This time there really was something wrong.* If there was one thing I had learned for sure over the years, it was: never judge a person's insides by their outsides.

"You probably just need to go to a few NA meetings, and get your life back on track." Those were the last words Dr PF had said to me.

The last meeting I had attended was the day before The Crash.

CHAPTER 4

Post-Crash

In the weeks after The Crash, I discover that writing off a Ferrari carries its own baggage, its own heavy weight. It's in a league of its own – very, very different to the consequences you may face if you, say, total an Uno or a Chevy Spark.

"It was an accident. These things happen. It's not like you woke up yesterday and said: 'Oh yes, today I am going to write off a Ferrari.'"

I am sitting, wracked in a heap of tears, in the boardroom of the Ferrari dealership on William Nicol, and the owner – a man who has every right to be angry – is trying to quietly comfort me.

"I'm sorry. I'm so sorry," I sob.

My whiplashed neck is in a brace, I can barely breathe – my ribs and chest ache from where the airbags shot out and bruised me. In a tear-blurred daze, I sign heaps of forms, fill in accident reports, recount the details. Somehow, I managed to open a case, at the Sandton police station, with the help of Boyfriend, a few hours after The Crash took place.

The woman dealing with the insurance at the Ferrari dealership tells me they have received CCTV footage of the incident, which they will examine. Footage? Oh my fuck! Where does that come from? She tells me that a business across the road has a permanent camera in position at the intersection. She is very reassuring. "You don't appear to be speeding. We should be okay. It looks like it's covered." She takes a very long pause. "You will, however, have to deal with the excess," she says, almost apologetically.

"The excess? But that's R32 000?" I whisper hoarsely. But I will deal with it, I decide. It's a lot of money, but I can make a plan.

"Uhmmm ... No, it's 10 per cent excess plus admin fees. That's R350 000."

Fuck. Fucking-fuck. That's the cost of a new 3-series. I go into a type of anaphylactic shock. I haven't eaten for 24 hours.

On the way back to the office, where I am to meet up with The Magazine publisher, the then editor – who is also my friend – plus the woman from HR, Boyfriend and I drive along the road I had travelled the day before, the day of The Crash. As we near the accident intersection, I can barely look. Metal and rubber debris litter the tar, the robot is still down, like a sentinel felled. Boyfriend turns the car around and heads down the road in exactly the same direction I was driving yesterday. "Think. Try to remember exactly what happened," he encourages me.

I force myself to stare into the eye of the oncoming storm. And then we see it. The overgrowth of a tree that obliterates all signs of an intersection approaching. He stops the car, turns around and we drive the route again. And there it is. A huge branch across the view of the robot, preventing a driver from seeing that a traffic light or an intersection lies ahead. This time I take pictures as we drive the route over and over again, trying to get the angle from the driver's perspective. I feel a small squeeze of relief. Maybe it wasn't all my fault. Maybe there's a perfectly legitimate explanation for why I simply didn't see the intersection. At this stage, all I am is confused.

The atmosphere in The Magazine's boardroom is vastly different to the one at the Ferrari dealership. While both the editor and publisher seem to be in shock, the HR woman appears to be in complete control. She spares no sympathy. "This is very, very serious," she says as she rattles off procedures: I am to provide a statement, as well as the accident report and case number, as soon as possible. As we leave the boardroom she finds a moment alone with me. "The company is going to get to the bottom of this." She also informs me that there will be some kind of disciplinary action.

What does this mean? I am terrified. "Am I going to lose my job? Get fired?" I ask, eyes huge.

"All I can tell you is that they are seeing this in a very serious light," I think I hear her say. "Gross negligence." Oh my god. My neck in the brace aches. I feel like my world is exploding. I can hardly breathe.

A blanket of doom settles over the office when I return to work. It seems that everyone in the entire building has heard about The Crash, and few of my colleagues are even talking to me. Whenever I walk into the canteen, it all goes dead quiet. The three passengers with me in the car are not yet back at work, and when they do return I suspect they have been told not to discuss the accident with me. I am desperate to make amends, but I don't quite know how – especially when no one's talking to me. The silence is unnerving. It feels like I am about to get the chop.

One afternoon I manage to catch a moment with the Food Ed. She is the only one with a visible injury, a line of tiny stitches crisscross her eyebrow. I crouch beside her at her desk, on my knees.

"I'm so, so sorry," I weep.

She opens her heart to me and receives me. Later she will tell me she too experienced The White Light when the Ferrari spun out of control.

Boyfriend advises me to get a lawyer. And, for a change, I don't argue. It's probably one of the most grown-up, self-loving things I have ever done for myself.

Owen, my attorney, is a small moonfaced beam of super energy with a brilliant legal mind. I have had a few contract negotiations with him over the years and he is the first legal person I think of. I leave a message on his voicemail.

It is over the final days of the Jewish holiday Sukkot – the

Festival of the Tabernacle – that Owen agrees to meet me for breakfast in Norwood. I unpack the events around The Crash, give him copies of the police statement and show him the pics of the accident scene. He tells me he will begin to start compiling a statement and forbids me to communicate another written word about the accident to the company unless he scrutinises it first. He is convinced the company is going to try to fire me and hold me liable for the R350 000 excess.

As we finish off our meeting I find myself telling him in detail what I experience during The Crash, when the car begins to career out of control and how a powerful white light comes down to bring the spinning metal to a stop. He remains silent for a while and then begins talk to me about Sukkot, in terms of the Kabbalah. He says, according to Kabbalah, absolutely nothing in this world exists outside of God. However, for us to have a human experience, most of the time God hides his infinite presence. So we go through life believing that ours is the true reality, and that God is somewhere out there, distant and separate from us.

"Around the time of Sukkot, this illusion begins to break down," he explains. "During this celebration we are supposed to build sukkah or some type of rectangular structure where we experience the existential truth and joy that we are not separate from God but within him. As we sit within the sukkah, we are sitting inside God."

He then says something that blows my mind. "The car you were driving at the time of the accident was a rectangular shape, a structure you had 'built' in the sense that you related deeply to it, in your materialistic, human experience. Your sukkah. I think what you experienced during the crash was a true Sukkot experience, where God showed himself – not to be something separate and apart from you, but right within you."

By the end of the story my eyes are streaming with tears. So are his.

Over the next 90 days, a long, drawn-out process begins to establish who is liable for the excess – me or the company. I am charged with gross negligence and served notice to attend a disciplinary hearing. This is a charge that carries with it the possibility of instant dismissal. I feel like my life and finances are hanging in the balance. There are times that I am so stressed that I drive both Boyfriend and my lawyer demented.

"You are one of the highest maintenance clients I have ever had," Owen blurts out at me in exasperation. I am not, however, one of his highest-paying ones, because by the end of the long, drawn-out case, he has charged me less than R10 000 for what could easily have been a bill of over R80 000 from any other lawyer.

Then, finally, on 2 December 2013, three months to the day after The Crash, I walk into the boardroom where my hearing is to take place. According to standard company law, because this is an internal process, I am not allowed to have legal representation. Although I am told I may have someone from within the company to defend me, it is clear that there is absolutely no one who can do this so I decide to represent myself.

I am well prepared, armed with a file of evidence, photographs and even a flip chart with diagrams of how the accident unfolded. The CCTV footage, saved on USB, is ready to be shown if need be. It effectively displays a discrepancy in when exactly the robot turned red, as well as showing the Ferrari moving to overtake slowly. In contrast, it shows the Pajero moving at a much higher speed.

I have spent most of the previous night with Owen at his office, putting the four pillars of my defence together. But as the night progresses I am so stressed that I can hardly breathe and I throw some irrational tantrum. Owen tells me to go home and get some sleep. He will send the rest of my defence later. When I wake up at 6 am my entire case is in my inbox.

In my best attempt to power dress and channel my no-nonsense *LA Law* look, I wear my Karen Millen pin-stripe suit. The day before, I have my hair done sleek and straight to mimic a let's-get-down-to-business look.

It turns out, I don't get fired. I get a final written warning and, when the time comes to pay a whopping bill of R650 000 – the owners of the Pajero had decided to weigh in with another

300k – the company comes to the table and pays. I will always be supremely grateful for their generosity.

But, as I'm about to find out, despite my money worries now finally over and my job still intact, post traumatic stress and all the fallout that comes with it is more insidious and a lot harder to deal with.

CHAPTER 5

The Weekend at the 7-Star Hotel

I said it all started with The Crash. But sometimes, when you look back at a powerful life-changing event that implodes, there are a whole bunch of mitigating factors that contribute to the actual explosion, the gunshot thwack, where the head cracks open like a big, pippy pomegranate.

So the actual *trigger* to me driving myself to the Hotel Hospital (in the Audi or the Alfa) was The Weekend. But the actual push-me-over-the-edge-of-the-cliff event had started six days earlier, before I checked in on Boyfriend on his birthday, April Fools' Day.

But for all of these events to have taken place, The Weekend of the Break-Up has to be considered a leading cause. This had happened six weeks earlier. At a seven-star luxury hotel.

It had come as a total shock. Cold and icy even though the night was sweltering.

You know those times when you don't see something until it hits you? Like a car accident, when you're left-sided by a truck or when you aquaplane across a wet road. When you swallow a bee from a can of fizzy drink at an airport, cut yourself on the jagged edge of a tin while you're feeding a homeless stray? That feeling when you get axed in the head from behind. Blood and guts of the heart stuff.

Just after Valentine's Day (not that we celebrated that commercial cheese – we were both too cool for that), I had taken Boyfriend to a seven-star mountain getaway an hour and half out of town. A PR team representing the marketing of the hotel had been on my case for ages, relentlessly pursuing me (plus partner) to stay for two nights. The trip offered all expenses paid, including full access to the mini bar, and couple's spa treatments. These were the obvious perks of working on a magazine. You get invited to things you could never normally afford, and get given gifts as veiled bribes in exchange for gushy editorial.

Of course, as "gratitude" for all the treats laid on, you're expected to review it. Favourably, of course. Travel and motoring journos are unarguably the biggest hos for freebies in the media industry. We might not earn huge amounts, but what we are rich in is experience.

Wealth used to be judged by the amount of money you managed to accumulate. But things have been changing ever since the world economic meltdown that kicked off with the collapse of the global bank Lehman Brothers in September 2008, an event that exposed the fragility of the world's economy and almost brought down the financial system of the entire planet.

As a result, today the world is regarded as a much less stable or predictable place. According to a recent life survey conducted by American Express, known as The Life Twist survey (due to the respondents' overwhelmingly similar attitudes towards the twists and turns they had come to expect in life), being regarded as successful no longer entails having money. In fact material wealth was right down at number 22 of 24 priorities in the survey. Having experiences such as happy relationships and adventures were regarded as by far the most important in order to have a fulfilled and successful life.

By all accounts, being afforded plenty of opportunity to travel and savour sponsored adventures and experiences, I appeared to be living *la vida loca*, the envy of my friends and acquaintances.

But, in reality, the majority of the time saw me playing in the playground of plastic.

Of course, most people would have immediately leapt at the opportunity to stay in a seven-star joint, but after almost a decade with The Magazine I had grown a strange aversion to the relentless hunters who called themselves PRs. I got a certain kick out of playing slippery cat-and-mouse games with them until they were salivating at the bit to have me agree to attend their launch or trip. Weird that I would get off on such pathetic power games but, shamefully, at that time I did. Looking back, I have come to believe the crappier you feel inside, the more you objectify and treat others badly.

Behind the scenes, me playing hard to get with the seven-star joint was utter bullshit on my part. I actually really didn't need that much convincing. I was close to finishing my fourth book on the stump-legged athlete and I was exhausted. So the intention behind the getaway was twofold: to share some much-needed romantic time (read: sex) with Boyfriend, and to get some quiet space to at least make some headway into writing the introduction and author's note for the book.

With matching his-and-hers Samsonite luggage packed, we were ready to leave by late Friday afternoon. We looked the perfect upwardly mobile seven-star couple as we drove into end-of-week get-out-of-town rush-hour traffic in the gorgeous new Jaguar XFR-S 5-litre, V8, 460kW, R1.4-million super sedan. With its 20-inch Varuna alloy wheels and Meridian sound system banging out the beats, my life felt pretty much complete. It's amazing how material objects can be such a seductive drug of denial and amnesia and how a Jag can make you forget a Ferrari, even if it's just for a few hours.

After checking in, we were taken in a golf cart to our VIP R7 000-a-night villa, perched on the edge of a never-ending smoky purple vista of mountains and valleys. The sweaty stiff-upper-lipped manager pointed out various high points: "The Jacuzzi is here, the mini bar here ... This is the WiFi code ... Breakfast is served from 7 am."

I wished he'd leave. I'd visited enough upscale joints to know where everything was. How hard was it going to be to find the kettle, for fuck's sake? In the end, besides minor décor details, all these swanky places looked pretty much the same. All I was really interested in was the damn WiFi code.

Fuck, I felt jaded. With the hotel man gone, surrounded by silence except for the whispering grass, and some faraway bird call, I found myself tumbling onto the triple king-size bed with 400-thread-count Egyptian linen.

Fuck, I was tired. I hadn't realised just how exhausted I really was. I half-heartedly shouted for Boyfriend, who was texting from a recliner on the deck of the plunge pool, to join me in the bedroom. He probably couldn't hear me. I didn't even have the energy to wonder who was taking up so much of his energy. Too tired to be curious, I made a mental note of it. It was a good line. "Too tired to be curious to care."

I closed my eyes and almost immediately drifted off into a deep slumber.

Boyfriend had been calling me narcoleptic for the past year. Maybe he was right, but I was usually asleep before he even got to -*leptic*. Truth be told, though, I was actually quite affronted by the label. There was nothing attractive about falling asleep all over the place – unless you were hot, like River Phoenix, of course. The only time I had ever come across an actual narco was River as Mickey, the half-asleep gay homeless hustler in *My Own Private Idaho*.

I loved that movie, especially River's character, who called himself a "connoisseur of roads" because he had been "tasting roads all [his] life". I guess he appealed to my sense of homelessness, never staying long enough in one place to allow grass to grow beneath my feet.

I remember when River died. It was September 1993. Just 23 years old, he had died of a speedball – a deadly cocktail of heroin and cocaine. Around that time I had just started playing around with smack – chasing the dragon. Melting sticky lines of brown heroin on silver tinfoil and inhaling the clouds of heady smoke through a foil tube. Despite being high as a kite, touching the clouds, I felt sad inside the day that River died. To help me forget, I lit another hit.

It was dark when I woke up in that king-size bed in the seven-star luxury hotel. I hated the grogginess you feel when you fall asleep at the wrong time, between that crack before day becomes night, and wake up feeling all wrong, like a chloroform cloud has invaded your brain.

The acrid smell of cigarette smoke that drifted in from the lounge area didn't help.

Fuck. The one thing management had requested was no smoking in the villa. I had stopped eight years ago and I wasn't one of those irritating non-smokers who held my nose and asked everyone else to abstain. Besides, I knew better than to ever say a word to Boyfriend when it came to his smoking. But still, right now I was the one responsible for the joint.

The blare of a Man United football match sliced through the silence.

I walked into the darkened lounge. He'd raided the mini bar, beer cans strewn all over the place. A bottle of red vintage wine stood open. R400 a pop. Merlot or Shiraz. It was too dark to tell.

"Darling? Uhmmm … Could you maybe smoke outside? You know, they asked me—"

"Fuck it!" he muttered, and hauled himself back onto the deck.

I hated that passive-aggressive thing he did.

"Okay, okay. Just not fight about it … Just calm down," my inner voice placated me. I would later christen her Echo. "You're here to rekindle the flames. Be nice to him. Put on that sexy little dress he gets hard for you in … and stop being so selfish. It's not all about you."

With Boyfriend, when all else failed, sex prevailed. We'd been together for almost nine years and the sex had never waned. Not one single bit. There was none of that usual bedroom boredom and tedium, that sense of being castrated by mundanity that often sets in between couples when you get to know each other inside and out. It was probably the most significant, and possibly even the only reason, why we were still together. I had never experienced anything quite like that in any of my previous relationships. Wasn't it supposed to be "familiarity breeds contempt"?

The great sex might have had something to do with the fact that we'd never moved in together, had never shared a common space. He stayed in his house and I stayed in mine. That's just the way he was. He had always been like that with girlfriends. Boundaries. Control. He was a "Treat them mean – keep them keen" kind of guy. After nine years of being together, I'd stopped thinking of it as weird. After nine years together, perhaps, I had lost the gift of discernment. Time can make a mockery of reason.

Although some of my friends in long-term relationships were envious of my verdant sex life, they definitely thought our living arrangement was strange. "When are you two going to move in together?" had become something of a mantra. I'd even stopped seeing most of them simply to avoid the questions.

But this was a first for me. This not-living-together thing.

I had always moved in with a dude, played housey-housey almost immediately with the man I "dated" and shagged. Looking back, some men who should have been one-night stands turned into four-year relationships because of immediate cohabitation. I had even married one. Boy 2 – the other one, the one who had been my husband.

But, unlike with Boyfriend, with all my live-ins, soon after the rose-tinted phase waned, we would slip into the creases in the couch. Watch television, slowly growing numb as the screen sucked all the passion and paused all the problems.

Then, finally, when a break-up was absolutely unavoidable – which was invariably long overdue – there'd be a screeching fight over fridges and coffee cups and knives and forks ... Dogs were especially hard when it came to the division of spoils. Never share an animal, I learned.

So maybe Boyfriend was right about keeping eroticism alive by not sharing common space. But if I were really honest, as the years passed, in the Quest for Flesh, the emotional intimacy between us floundered below zero. It was all about priorities, he'd tell me. Keeping the erotic going required tactics of destabilisation.

A while back he had suggested that I read *Mating in Captivity*, a book by Esther Perel. Perel wrote that the reason why couples stop shagging is because, in modern-day relationships, we are expected to be both best friend and erotic partner. According to Perel, the two simply don't mix. Once couples move in together, get to know each other, become "best friends" and lose the edge, desirability and sexual sparks go south. Living together, she says, kills desire, the whole "familiarity breeds contempt" philosophy. Couples get hooked on security, knowing each other totally, expecting their partners to know them completely. They look to each other and expect that each one will make the other feel whole, that they own and belong to each other. There is no gap for discovery, no surprise and, as a result, all desire is lost.

Perel goes on to question the real connection between love and desire. How do they conflict and not mix with each other? She comes up with an interesting conclusion. The verb that comes with love is to *have* and the verb that comes with desire it is to *want*. In other words, *love* is all about being close, knowing everything about the beloved, narrowing the stranger gap, obliterating the tension. Whereas when we are in a state of *desire*, we don't want to know the end. We don't have a sense of comfort or conclusion. With desire, we sense the adventure, the unknown; there's an edge, a modicum of insecurity ...

So it was that, in a weird just-woken-up haze of automation, I made my way back to the bedroom and took out my black sexy stockings and fuck-me heels. In the bathroom, I slipped on my little black dress, looked at myself in the mirror. I think I liked what I saw, but I wasn't even sure of that. I looked tired. My reflection blurred before my eyes. My body morphed in and out of shape. At the time, I was a size 8. But, with my Body Dysmorphic glasses on, that could easily balloon into a size 12. I had to work fucking hard to keep it that way. Thin. Not too long ago, I had actually been a size 12 and I had even been a size 14 at one point.

"Sizeist," the voice snarled.

It was true. I was obsessed by size. My own body shape had been tormenting me since I was a child. Growing up with an overweight older sister had elicited dread and terror in me. Additionally, a hugely critical mother always kept an eye on our weight and watched the contents of the fridge like a beady-eyed Nazi mouse. I have never forgotten the year her idea of a birthday present to my sister came in the form of a Weight Watchers diet plan, wrapped up in an envelope and tied with a bow.

By the age of 14 I was dieting insanely, shedding kilos like a moulting cat. Thin meant I was good, fat meant I was a failure. Dieting and deprivation became part of my everyday life, after waking up and before going to sleep, assessing whether I had been a "good" or a "bad" girl. But with serial dieting came starvation and a crazy desire to stuff my face. At least that's how it was for me. Then, in order to stave off the inevitable weight gain and the insane sugar craving that comes from crash dieting, I began my long journey with Mistress Binge-and-Purge, otherwise known as Bulimia.

Of all the substances to which I have been addicted – and there have been many: heroin, crack, alcohol, dagga, ecstasy and nicotine – food has probably been the most deviant and the hardest to handle; sugar specifically, but actually food in all shapes, textures and flavours.

And if I was sizeist, Boyfriend was too – brutally so. It was thus quite logical that it would be on his watch that I'd lose the 15 kilos I'd accumulated over a period of about two years.

The weight gain had started surreptitiously after I'd stopped smoking – just when I had met him. That was during a crazy, dark time in my life when, within three days of kicking the nicotine, I'd learned that my mother was dying of pancreatic cancer. At the time I most needed the crutch of a Camel, I tossed it aside. But in ditching the cigarettes, I reached for food and the kilos began to pile on.

At first I hadn't even noticed really, but slowly, like a devious fog creeping in, the jeans I'd previously slipped effortlessly into no longer fit that easily around the hips, struggling to close at the waist.

So I began to avoid certain outfits. I told myself that a too-hot wash was the reason the skirt was now too tight. When I tried on clothes in a store and realised I needed a bigger size, I blamed the new sizing systems. I stopped looking in the mirror, afraid of what I'd see, which was hard for me, because from the time I was little I had been kind of obsessed with my reflection.

When I asked Boyfriend whether I looked fat in an outfit, he would half grin and say: "What d'you think, Tubby?" Tubby! What kind of a fucking name was that? I kept my anger inside, of course – and reached for an extra helping of dessert instead.

Then one day I went to a doctor for something quite arbitrary. As part of the routine check-up, I was told to get on the scale and I weighed a whopping 75 kilos. Since giving up the cigarettes, I had put on 17 kilogrammes of flab. For someone my height, that was insane. How had that happened without me even noticing? I wept all the way home. Now each time I looked in the mirror a pale, puffy Bridget Jones stood before me, all plump and distended around my hips, ass and boobs. I hated what I saw. My outsides told me what an abject failure I was.

I now attacked my body mercilessly, willing and beating it into submission according to my grand plan. My gym membership, which had been on the verge of expiry, was suddenly reactivated. Cardio, in the form of spinning, became my daily ritual. I tried to cut out sugar and began to eat almost entirely vegetarian, which was easy because Boyfriend was a great veggie cook.

The scale became my daily companion. Every morning my worth greeted me by way of my weight in numbers. And slowly, over the next few months, the kilos melted away and by the end of that year I was back to a svelte me. I made a pact never to let my eye off the ball again.

And then one day, about a year before I admitted myself to Hotel Hospital, driving home from a particularly stressful day at The Magazine, I had a deep and inexplicable craving for something sweet. It was such an utterly overwhelming longing that it forced me to pull over at the service station around the corner from my home. Like a drugged-up zombie, I walked up and down the sweet aisles, surveying the display rows of Kit Kats, Tempos and Bar

Ones. And then I reached the ice-cream fridge. Shiny ice-cream wrappers glinted back at me. Armed with my Almond Magnum, it felt like I had scored a gram of the best crack in town. By the time I got home it was finished.

The next day it happened again. And the next and the next and the next. By the end of the week, one ice cream had become two, adding the Classic to my Almond stash. I think one day I ate five. Sickly sweet icky sugar filling that hole in my soul that was suddenly getting a whole lot bigger.

Sugar had become my new addiction, my stress reliever, my surrogate mommy. It felt comforting knowing that I had something to rely on on dark and lonely days.

But on the flip side, the fear of ballooning, putting all that weight back on, screeched at me. I had already seen the scale's needle move up two notches since my foray into ice cream. There was only one thing to do: get rid of it. And so, just as a fraudster deletes all evidence of the crime, I needed to remove all trace of my failing as soon as possible.

And so I found myself back with my head down the toilet bowl. The quick-and-easy "you can have your cake and eat it" solution. When things got really stressful – like after The Crash, or after The Weekend – I found my sugar craving to be as strong as my darkest days on heroin and crack.

By the time I booked into Hotel Hospital, in the week leading up to my self-admission, I had been fixing on sugar day and night.

At the seven-star luxury getaway, I avoided the sweets in the mini bar fridge. Instead I stared back at my reflection in the mirror in the bathroom while Boyfriend puffed away on the deck. It had become a habit of mine. Looking at myself. It reminded me that I was alive. On the outside I liked what I saw. On the inside I'd never been so lonely in my life.

I felt a bit like a Glock without a round – a bit like that Kid Cudi song that bounced around in my brain.

I checked my hip bones one more time and added a slick of matte red lipstick. Danger Red. Mac.

I went out to where he sat under the stars. He didn't look up. He was still texting. In retrospect, I should have grabbed his phone there and then to find out who was keeping him so distracted. Instead I sidled closer.

Hardly noticing me at all, wine glass in hand, he moved straight past me and back inside. Man U had resumed their game after halftime. I had learned never to seek attention during a football match, so I sat on the couch opposite, waiting on the sidelines practising my best Stepford Wife glare.

When the final whistle blew I dug the heel of my fuck-me shoe into his crotch. He usually loved it when I did that. But this time he barely noticed. He got up abruptly, and moved outside again for another smoke. I hated it when he did that. Chose cigarettes, little nicotine sticks, over me.

"Play with yourself," he commanded from the deck, muttered like a crumpled-up afterthought. I wasn't really in the mood for masturbation. I had come all this way, made all this effort, to feel some skin. Suck his cock. Cum. Fuck.

I suddenly felt a wave of sleepiness wash over me. Jeez. Maybe I *was* a River Phoenix narco. Stay the fuck awake! I pinched myself. I forced myself up, moved to the deck. I sat on his lap, rubbing myself on his hardening crotch. He touched my breasts. He never could resist my tits. I leaned in closer. He pulled the straps down, his mouth finding my hardening nipples. I felt him get harder. God, I loved his cock. Then I was in the place he liked most. On my knees I unzipped him and went down on him, looking up. The way he loved it. Slowly. Gently, then all the way Down. It left me breathless. I felt him relax, close his eyes. I felt my worth rise as my mouth sucked and stroked his rock-hard cock. And all the erotic tension grew in the ink-black star-speckled night. And in all that alienated separation, desire returned.

* * *

He didn't cum and neither did I that night.

A little later I went to the bedroom to fetch a jersey, found myself on the Egyptian cotton duvet, lay down for what I told myself would be five minutes and woke up three hours later as he bumped into the side table on his way inside. I could hear by the way he moved that he had made further inroads into the mini bar.

He smelt of whiskey and smoke.

He stumbled slightly and switched on the aircon. Like open-plan offices, the other thing I hate is fucking aircon.

"Please turn it off," I groaned. He snarled under his breath. Through sleep-foggy eyes I watched him pull the heavy double-layer floor-length curtains open.

"Noooooooooo! Please keep them closed," I whinged. "I need to sleep late. The light will wake us too early."

That was it. Out of the room he stormed, and back to the deck. Sleep-bleary, I followed him.

"Darling, please don't be cross ... Please come to bed. I didn't mean that. I miss you – I want you. I'm sorry. You can put the aircon on – please come back."

He stayed silent. I could feel his fuming. He poured another glass. Lit a cigarette. Fuck.

"Why don't you come in? Please. Don't you think you've had too much to drink?" As soon as the words left my mouth I wished I could retract them, unpull the trigger. The unleashing, the rushing avalanche. It was as if what would follow had been bubbling under for a thousand years, waiting, longing, to explode.

"Okay, that's it! That is fucking it. It's over, it's over! Do you fucking hear me? It's over." His voice burst thunder into the ink-black sky.

Over? Over-over? WTF? Over aircon ...? Curtains?

"Darling, please ..." I could feel a panic attack begin to rise within me.

"No, no, no! I mean it. This is it – it's over. You and I are done! We're totally incompatible ... You like all this crap – this five-star-hotel bullshit. I hate all of this. I like camping ... The outdoors. I want to be out *there*" – he pointed at the faraway shapes of dark mountains. "I don't wanna be here. It's over. We've had a good run ... Nine years – that's more than I have ever spent with anyone, but now we're done."

And all I could say was: "But why didn't you say something before? After nine years, you've only noticed now?"

Then I began to weep.

That was end-February. By the first week of April my tears had become the Red Sea.

And, as with everything in this world – cliché as it is – there's always a price to pay. Desire gone wrong often results in chaos and madness.

CHAPTER 6

The Birthday Party

It's no coincidence that almost all self-help books advise you not to sleep with your ex. The main reason probably has something to do with this: hell hath no fury like a woman who's just been dumped.

Over the decade that I worked at The Magazine, I often found myself espousing "deep" relationship literature, writing scenarios that weigh up the pros and cons of shagging the ex:

So the relationship has ended and most of the belongings, pet arrangements and money issues have been sorted out. Then one night, just as you've stopped checking his Facebook page and WhatsApp timeline, to spy on when he was last online, he calls you and invites you over for dinner, offering to make you that mushroom risotto you loved so much. Your heart races – sure, you loved the risotto but it's the idea of physical proximity that's getting your adrenaline pumping. You tell yourself it's a good idea because you want to get that book Return to Love, *by Marianne Williamson, back – the one you lent him to heal his soul, hoping he would get some guidance to get more emotionally connected to you. But, deep down, you know you have really accepted the invitation because you're feeling goddamn lonely. You can't bear another Friday night watching reruns of* The Walking Dead. *As you drive on the familiar streets you've driven so many times on the way to his house, the memories start flooding back: you're right in the loop, back in dangerous territory. The dog goes mental when he sees you, the ex's smell intoxicates you as you give him a friendly hug. Before dinner you go to the bathroom to check for new toothbrushes, lingerie stuffed in the linen basket, lipstick, mascara – any telltale signs of a new bitch on the block. You find nothing. You're relieved. Goddamn it, your heart is beating double time – there's no one new. Yet. You inhale deeply, spray a quick whiff of Issey Miyake from the bottle you gave him last birthday.*

Over dinner you're on your best, most engaging behaviour. You're funny, lighthearted; you're interested in everything he says. You praise each home-cooked morsel that you eat, the conversation flows – you begin to wonder why you two ever called it quits. And before you know it, you're back in the passion zone, your clothes are hanging off the lampshades and you're shagging all over the place. Goddamn, this feels so, so right.

"Don't worry," I've told my readers countless times, in every regurgitated "Breaking up with your ex" story I've ever written, "you're not alone". No sweat, say the relationship self-help gurus, this is a common occurrence. Humans love to return to familiar places, even if you've had an acrimonious break up.

And you don't have to be a brain surgeon to get why. Basically, at the end of the day, we all have a desire to feel connected to someone we know. Then there's the power game element – if he rejected you it makes sense that you might try to manipulate him into getting back together, just to feel better about yourself so you can gain back the power you lost, not only in the relationship, but in the break-up. Then, of course, there's shagging ... Why go through all that god-awful discomfort of looking for someone new when you can have your sexual needs met without having to actually go out and look for a replacement? Plus, you get an immediate, albeit short-term, fix that boosts your self-esteem, and reassures you that you're still desirable.

After the weekend at the luxury getaway (which would later become known as Heartbreak Hotel), Boyfriend and I parted ways. He went to his home and I went to mine. I have to admit that I suddenly saw some logic in his "you play at yours and I'll play at mine" theory. No belongings to be divided, no financial tugs of wars, no animals to bicker over. I did ask him for my new Iain Banks book, as well as my Richard Dawkins and Patrick Holford's *How to Quit Without Feeling Shit*. (I hoped there was a chapter on withdrawing from men.) I'm not sure how my collected poems of Sylvia Plath landed there. He hated dark, suicidal women poets – in fact, I was beginning to believe that he pretty much hated women in general – but I got my Plath back too. I told him to chuck the toothbrush. It was bristled anyway. I kept his favourite sleep shorts, the tatty ones he had once left at my place. I'm not sure why.

And that was it: clean, clear and clinical.

At least that's how it appeared on the surface.

Inside I was screaming. My entire world had fallen apart. For nine years he had been with me, at my side, in my head, in my bed.

Now that it was over, I was amazed at how I immediately found myself gravitating towards whitewashing him. Making him the patient, long-suffering, loving boyfriend, who had been available and loving to me through thick and thin.

I kept thinking back on how, right through my mother's cancer diagnosis, during the year of my mother's dying, he had been at my side. Writing my first book, *Smacked*, he had willed me on right to the end, through those last 20 000 words. Then came *Hooked*. And even though I slagged him off in it, he stuck by me, right to the very last word. Then I wrote my third (on fallen township princess Kelly Khumalo, the one who was seeing soccer captain Senzo Meyiwa when he was gunned down at her home in 2014). He shot the cover image of Kelly, all gorgeous and glam, where she looked like an exotic Spanish Hollywood diva in purples and pinks, as well as all the images inside. He travelled halfway across the country with me to interview Kelly in Ntinini, the rural village in northern KwaZulu-Natal where she grew up in poverty and hardship. He read through my words, cooked me meals and, shag-wise, he was the only man I had met so far who had managed to keep me in lust from day one until the end.

But once I finally lifted those rose-tinted specs from my love-impaired eyes, I started to see how in reality the relationship had been in crisis for years. Me deciding to bury myself in my two-year Honours degree in Publishing at Wits, attending classes twice a week, doing assignments late into the night, waking up at 3 am on weekends to write, work and study, were all just ways to avoid the truth that things between us were pretty well fucked up.

I should have seen that things were unravelling irrevocably when I found myself falling asleep on the couch at 7 pm as he cooked dinner. The tiredness grew in me like some wild rampant fungus. The narcolepsy was no longer even a joke – it was happening more and more frequently. Why did I not hear alarm bells ringing when I found myself fast asleep before he even got into bed? There were even a few times I dropped off while we were shagging.

Even our strongest area of connection was becoming tainted. We were a goddamn mess.

And while I toiled and twisted, working harder and harder, getting distinctions for my assignments and collecting words for my book like breeding butterflies, the more I buried myself in work, the more he receded and the more he began to drink and drink and drink.

While he stewed in spirit-induced silence, resentments growing like a carpet of mycelium, I worked and worked and worked, oblivious of the axe that was about to fall, a guillotine that would rent my world apart. God, I wish I had been more vigilant, more honest with myself about our downward spiral.

And yet, after it all ended, the only words that remained and bounced around my brain were the insults he hurled at me that night: "selfish", "self-obsessed", "narcissistic" and "insane".

It was all my fault. I took it all on myself and let those knives cut me to the core. I was a jellyfish, compliant. And dead.

I soon fell into a tunnel of self-recrimination. How could I have been so stupid? So unaware of his needs? How could I not have seen it, the break-up coming like ominous storm clouds gathering on the horizon? Surely I should have noticed the signs. Was I so out of touch, so caught up in my me-me-me world, so brainwashed by some Hollywood delusion, that I had lost the ability to reason and see? It was the last thing I expected – the axe that came down and chopped my little red heart into a million tiny pieces.

It was only much later, once those eyes that spilled with tears for weeks had dried, only after I had spent 21 whole days at the Hotel Hospital, that I would eventually emerge from the long sleep of self-flagellation and denial and begin to see how his accusations didn't totally wash. Weren't people who loved each other supposed to stick it out and support one another? Talk it over, walk through the bad times, in "sickness and in health"?

It's not as though he had been some kind of saint. It's not as if there hadn't been plenty of brutal times with him too: the two trips to casualty when a spider bite became so infected that it nearly took chunks out of his left arm. And then the time, less than a year back, when he'd climbed out of bed, walking in his sleep across the gantry that connected the bedroom to the rest of the split-level house, down the stairs and punched himself in a mirror – he had suddenly woken up and seen the reflection of himself, which he had mistaken to be the face of an intruder. Jung would have had a field day with this. I mean, how fucked up was that, attacking one's own reflection? I should have taken a step back then, run out of the door and down the street when I was confronted with the mess downstairs, blood pouring from his arms and ankle, like a scene from *The* fucking *Shining*.

Instead of running, I'd hauled him to casualty, and while he was being stitched up I'd returned to the "crime scene" to face the *Scream 1, 2* and *3* bloodbath. I had spent two hours mopping up his bright red gore, which had spread from the kitchen to the other side of the lounge. I'd gathered the towels, sheets and clothes seeped in crimson and made sure they were washed by the time he came home. Surely scrubbing away someone's blood counted for at least three of my transgressions: writing a book, studying and falling asleep before he fucked me? Surely my blood efforts counted for something?

And then, of course, there was his drinking. The promises to stop. The regular 90 days of white-knuckled abstinence followed by a fast downslide into extremes, which meant starting the day with a quick nip of vodka in the morning and ending the night with a clutch of empty wine bottles strewn across the room. The drinking that should have sent me packing, but instead kind of numbed me, making me feel like I was part of something weirdly familiar, reminding me of my years as a child, growing up alongside a mother who would also end each night soaked in alcohol.

Let's not forget about the two stints in rehab, the other women – two I knew of, but who knows whether there were others. It always felt like there was an intruder hanging around somewhere in the ether of our bed. Surely all of these counted for at least The Crash and my second book? So after weighing up all of this, all the "You did that"s and "I did this"s, at most I probably owed him two books' worth of support. Surely we could work things out?

Besides, I had been getting a growing feeling that the break-up was not as clean cut as it initially appeared to be. The first thing I had asked him that night on the deck when he announced the end was: "Is there another woman? Is there someone else?" Deep in my gut I was certain there was. I knew him well enough. It seemed highly unlikely that he would break it off with me unless he had a fallback girl. He was incapable of living without tits and a cunt in his life.

But he had laughed the notion off. "I have been in relationships since I was 16," he said. "Women have held me hostage and dominated my life ever since I can remember. I want to be free of the bitches and give myself a chance. Without all the drama."

In the heat of the moment, that sounded fair enough; I desperately wanted to believe I was not being chucked away for another. I needed to believe that. And so I breathed easier. Short, sharp intakes, mind you. No *pranayama* yogi breathing.

The following morning we packed up our things and drove away from the seven-star luxury in separated silence. He brought my books over that evening and the puppy, for a night, to "keep me company". I was not impressed. I loved the puppy but having her beside me only made my heart bleed more.

Then, after a few days, the WhatsApps began. It still made my heart beat every time I saw his name.

Because sex had been our meeting point throughout the relationship, it seemed logical that we would continue shagging. We did it once and it was as hot as ever, so we agreed to do it once a week. It was usually a Friday. Friends with benefits ... I had written and read countless stories about this arrangement. The only demand I made was that he promise that, if he met someone else, he would tell me. I really didn't want to be involved in some seedy triangle. Plus, of course, there were diseases. Honesty and transparency – that really didn't seem like too tall an order. He assured me that he would comply.

The month of March dawned, and our passion for each other in bed didn't abate – in fact, if anything, it just got more intense. We knew each other like the route you take home. We knew what our bodies liked, how they would instantly melt and slide into each other. I knew how to get him hard in less than 15 seconds. Like getting the roof of a 4-series Cab down. I would be turned on before I even arrived at his place, before he even touched me.

We began to see each other more; now it became twice a week. It had begun to feel like we were slowly slipping back into the rabbit hole of Us. Like nothing had changed. Since there had hardly ever been any really deep emotional stuff between us, the sex cemented us back together. We didn't need to discuss what we were feeling, because our bodies had returned to that place of familiar pleasure. The memory of the break-up receded, became vague. In my head it had begun to feel like we had never parted.

At the beginning of April he decided to throw a birthday dinner for about 10 people at the Taiwanese place in the Chinese district that we used to frequent. The day before the party, we made arrangements that I would spend the night with him after the dinner; it would be his "birthday treat to fuck me", he said. In addition to the promise of a night filled with sex, I gave him a set of beautiful grey cotton sheets. We could christen them that night, I wrote in the birthday card.

I couldn't wait. I felt special and loved and wanted. I even managed to squeeze in an unscheduled wax, I wore my best red dress, and my long hair got GHDed shiny for the occasion, just the way he liked it. I wanted him to look at me and regret the day he tore us asunder.

It was a Wednesday night and by the time I arrived the other guests were already there. I hadn't realised he had so many friends – where the hell had he found time to meet all these new people? I grabbed the empty chair next to him; it felt like it had been kept open especially for me. It felt good to stake out my territory.

The three lesbians from next door were opposite us at the table. The two who were a couple greeted me warmly, the third – an ageing redhead Dutch woman – gave me a clear miss. I glared at her. Why the fuck was she giving me attitude? Our paths had crossed on a previous occasion, a few months earlier when I unexpectedly dropped past Boyfriend's house in the middle of the day. As I pulled up, I could have sworn she had just walked down his drive. It was a confusing moment. She climbed into the car without so much as greeting me. I was taken aback, and remember thinking she looked somewhat hungover.

"What the fuck is wrong with that Dutch trash bag?" I had asked him.

"Oh, just ignore her – she's an unfriendly cow to everyone."

I hadn't given her a second thought. Except when, a week later, I noticed a new painting on his kitchen wall – a disastrous, red mishmash of a bloody-faced woman.

"Where the fuck did you get this thing?" I had asked.

"Oh, it's the Dutch lesbian's. She asked me to store some of her paintings in the garage."

"So why is it up here? God, it's fucking ugly. Do you really have to have it right above where we eat?"

He had made up some vague reason that this one needed special storage blah blah blah.

A week later it was still here.

Now in the restaurant, across the round table, she was glaring at me from her piggy alcohol-bleary eyes. I turned away and began playing the sweet wifey-wife, helping Ex-Boyfriend take the food orders. There were a mixture of carnivores and vegetarians and, like a good hostess, I made sure there was enough of a variety of food to please all palates. In order to be extra nice, I even ordered the somewhat absurdly named vegetarian prawns for the Dutch lesbian and the other grass feeders. The food soon began to arrive. As the plates were served I double-checked with the Taiwanese waitress what was what. The pile of vegetarian prawns was sent down to the Dutch lesbian's side. From across the table I heard her begin to wax lyrical about how good they were. "I haf had dese before – dey are delishush ..."

Ten minutes later the next round of dishes arrived.

"What are these?" I asked a new waitress.

"Vegetarian prawns," she said emphatically.

Oh fuck a duck. "So what was on the other plate?" I pointed across the table. The guests had suddenly grown ghostly quiet.

"That must have been the chicken, Madame."

I tried to swallow back a giggle. The table was silent. The Dutch lesbian looked ill. She had just chewed her last "prawn".

"Oh dear. Oh fuck, I'm so sorry," I announced across the table. "There seems to have been some mistake. Whoever ate the veggie prawns, it looks like you ate the chicken." Gulp. I could not hide my grin. That would serve the bitch right. So much for being this authentic veggie lover.

Ex-Boyfriend didn't appear to be too fussed. By that point, he was well into a second bottle of wine, some saki and a few Chinese beer chasers. For the rest of the night I continued to be firmly implanted at his side while the Dutch lesbian glowered from the opposite side of the table.

When it came time to leave, Ex-Boyfriend and I walked past the Dutch newly turned carnivore. She was standing outside on the dingey corner that smelt of cat piss, lost and forlorn. I shouted goodbye to no one in particular. I was the queen of the night.

As always, the sex when we got back to his home was *good*:

dirty and debauched in all the right places. Later, after our almost two-hour session, he was downstairs fetching water when the post-coital silence was broken by the tinkle of a WhatsApp message on his phone. 12:35 am. Strange time for someone to be texting. Weird how the throb of suspicion sounds: loud, like a wake-up gong in a Tibetan monastery. It had that "you need to read this" ring to it. My hand reached out for his Samsung.

Now, it's not as if I was a stranger to snooping, stalking, sneaking a peek at messages … I had broken into his phone many times over the years. But even I, in my delirious denial, knew that somehow this time I was treading shaky ground. We had broken up, I had no rights, nada – no recourse whatsoever. But, of course, that didn't stop me. I needed to move quickly; I could sense he would be back any minute. Miraculously, I broke the security password code first time. It was as if I had been given the cue by the hacker gods.

And there it was.

"So, did I play my part well tonight?"

I looked for a name. Lotte.

The Dutch prawn-loving lesbian's name cackled back at me.

The words stung my retinas. Immediately I sensed there was devious intention written all over the cunt's cryptic eight-word text.

My mind raced to establish meaning.

I needed more proof to back up my suspicions. Quickly.

I scrolled back to earlier messages. My heart beat fast, almost busting out of my sternum.

"Would you like a massage, sexy? I have baby oil with me."

Right. Next one. Quick – I could sense he was coming.

"Open up. I am downstairs."

That one was sent at 11 pm three nights earlier. I doubt she was coming over for tea.

Then I heard footsteps approaching, up the stairs. My heart was racing a million beats per second. I barely had time to replace the phone before he re-entered the room, two glasses of water in hand.

I lounged back casually, trying to channel my laid-back Delilah.

"So, did I play my part well tonight?" Had I inadvertently

switched to a Dutch accent? I steadied myself.

The words hung in the air like an unwanted dwarf baby.

He looked taken aback, like he honestly had no idea what I was on about.

"So, did I? Play my part well, I mean."

Now he was getting irritated.

"What do you think someone would mean if they asked you that?" I continued to set my trap.

Still nothing.

The suspense became unbearable, threatening to choke me. I had to do it, reveal my ace, show him what was up my sleeve. I was never too good at playing my cards close to my chest. I reached for the phone and shoved it in his face.

"Read that."

All hell broke loose – as it usually does when someone has something to hide, goes into denial.

"What the fuck are you doing with my phone? Who gave you the fucking right? You have so crossed the line. You need to leave; you need to leave now! Now!" Blah blah blah.

It was so obvious what was going on. Suddenly, everything made sense: her walking down his drive, the bad vibes and glaring daggers, her god-awful mishmash of a painting in his kitchen, hung up in there like some kind of fuck-me trophy, her poison stares at the birthday dinner, the endless texting on the deck the weekend of the break-up. Of fucking course. Why hadn't I seen it? It was all so blatantly fucking clear now.

It was too cold and too late to leave. I fell asleep shivering. The following morning I skulked out before the sun rose.

CHAPTER 7

The Fractured Penis Weekend

The big reveal birthday had been on the Wednesday. By Friday I was obsessed, my mind doing cartwheels, tapeworms devouring all sanity and reason. I could not let go of the idea of him and her together. Over and over. Pictures spinning round and round my head. Sleep completely evaded me. Just endless sick Dutch porno movie snippets playing over and over.

At 4 am on Saturday morning I had a deep, dark urge to get into my car and see it for myself. I thought that by confronting the source of my pain in full 3D Technicolor I would miraculously find release from the agony. Finally, by 5:30 am, I had grown too weary to resist the voice that kept urging me on. In order to give myself an alibi of sorts, I decided to send a text message, asking him whether I could come over and retrieve my charger, which was still plugged into the socket on what used to be my side of the bed. After all, a girl needs a charger, doesn't she? In reality, I had plenty of spares, of course. It was a weak, obviously crap reason, but it was the best I could come up with in my current state of mind. There was no response to my text. I got into the car – I think it was the Golf 7, the one that should have won the

Car of the Year in 2013 – and headed down to his place.

The street was silent as I parked the VW. I still had keys to his house, so my intrusion seemed rather civilised, almost as if I had the right to break in and enter. The steps leading to his second-storey split-level house had never seemed as steep as I heaved my heavy heart towards the door. I didn't have to unlock anything as everything was wide open, music blaring out across the valley. Six in the morning and the place sounded like a club in Ibiza.

The first thing I noticed as I neared the wide-open glass doors leading into the lounge was a woman's jersey on the couch on which he and I had shagged so many times. It hung casually across the backrest; it cooed in comfort.

And so I crossed the threshold. There was no turning back now.

Then I saw him. He didn't see me. He wore a leather Nazi-type coat – and nothing else. He was swaying to the music, dreads hanging all the way down his back.

I stood frozen. The shock on his face as he turned toward me was memorable.

"Kitttttyyyy," the alcohol from an all-nighter fumed heavy on his breath, his plastered grin like a newly laid wreath on a marble tombstone.

"The charger – I sent you a message. I need it …" My voice petered out.

"I'll get it," he stumbled. He was far too slow for sober little OCD me.

"No! I will!"

I had pre-empted the move and, in a flash, had kicked off my black Fitflop shoes – ones I had been given to review a few months earlier – and scaled the ladder to the bedroom loft two rungs at a time. And even though I'm terrified of heights, I made it up to the top, across the gantry and into the bedroom – *our* bedroom – in less than a flash.

And there, on the pillow, strewn out across where I had laid my head for many years – in fact, just three days earlier – was a shock of died orange hair, a stain of colour against the pillowcase: the gift I had just bought him. The face and body were tucked somewhere under the duck-down duvet.

My breath slowed. Like a panther stalking its prey, I moved in slow-motion silence towards the charger still hanging like a slack cock from the socket in the wall.

As I got closer to her head, my breathing slowed right down to barely imperceptible. This was my glorious Glenn Close moment. All that was missing was a pair of scissors to cut her into pieces. I suddenly understood what lay behind a crime of passion because in that moment I could so easily have plunged a knife through the covers, punctured the bitch full of holes. The power I felt right there was unforgettable.

I found him on the balcony surveying the pale orange sunrise, glass of insipid pink rosé in hand. He had a grin plastered across his face, like some dumb hyena that had just finished up at a kill. But underlying the mock of normality, there was an edge of discomfort that hung thick in the air. I would like to think that right in that moment he knew he was a cunt.

"I think you need to give my keys back," he said. Deadpan.

Fuck the fucker. And then it came in torrents, it all came pouring out.

"You fucking liar, you broke the deal! You were supposed to tell me. You promised you would! We said if anyone else came along we would tell each other ..."

And then the Furies were upon me, flames of justice and vengeance streaking through my mind, jolting me out the chair like some Abu Ghraib shock torture therapy. Now I was running right back up the ladder two rungs at a time, leaving him behind with the same grin on his face. Up to the top, across the wooden gantry, back into the room to the bed where we had lain for almost 10 long years. Her box-red hair stopped me in my tracks; it spread out on the grey pillowcase like a gash of blood, a fan of Medusa snakes, a terrible secret uncovered. Like a thousand pointing fingers mocking me ...

Then I was almost on top of her, my mouth covering her ear like a psycho shell, the screech from within rising from that ancient place of rage, the place of bones and skulls a million years old.

"FUUUUUCCCKKKKKKKEEERRRRR! WAAAKE THE FUCCCKKK UP! GET THE FUCKKKKKKK OUT OF MY BED!"

Her ashen alcohol-soiled face crumpled out from beneath the covers, grunting like a goat.

"Get out of my bed, you cunt!" I hissed. "These sheets – these are my sheets, you dumb bitch. I gave them to him for his birthday. I came all over them on Wednesday! You are lying in my cum! Get OUT! OUT!"

And then it was over, the bullet of rage spent from the chamber. Out of body, I watched myself from the ceiling – pathetic little me, trash-bag she. And I knew I needed to go.

The rush of sadness almost drowned me.

The tears flew as I stumbled backwards, across the gantry, repelled by what I had done, by what I had become in that space pocket of insanity. I almost fell down the last four rungs of the ladder.

He still had the same look on his face as I sobbed my way back past him. He was loving it, the drama, the chaos. I needed to leave. Get away.

And then, in crumpled black, she was behind me, stumbling out onto the balcony.

"Where you going? Stay," he slurred at her. I threw his keys back at him.

I opened the door to the Golf 7. It had started to rain. I turned the key in the ignition. I reversed out and drove down the road, zero to 100 in 6.2 seconds. I don't know how I got back home.

* * *

I began to clean the house, trying to find traces of him and Hoover them away. I made a bowl of popcorn, and gulped down two litres of Coke Zero, felt sick and then chucked it all up. I went onto Facebook and told my 5 000 friends how happy I was. There were 72 likes in the first 10 minutes.

At around 13:30 I heard keys in my front gate. Just as I had broken in and entered earlier, he came in through the front door without an invitation. His six-foot-seven frame filled the room as he laid down a bunch of "gifts". Among them a first edition of my book *Smacked*, a piece of tourmaline stone and a pair of velvet trousers.

"Try them on, Kitty – I'm not sure if they're your size."

He was acting as if nothing had happened. I felt as if I had been going out of my mind, but how could I resist a sleek, sexy-looking skin-tight pair of trousers? In that Body Dysmorphic moment, all my resolve to vacuum him away went out the window.

Then, as I tugged the trousers over my ass, I felt him up behind me. His hard-on was raging. It didn't take much for the new outfit to be on the floor as he took me from behind thrusting into me … and just as had so often happened when it came to him, all my sensibilities flew out the window. And then, in a moment of high desire, just as he was heading for the home run, it happened:

CRACK. THWACK.

His rock-hard penis thrust back and hit me, full blunt force, on the sacrum just above the coccyx and it snapped. Like a pretzel stick. THWACK! Just like that.

Almost immediately blood burst into the sac, causing his testicles to swell to double their size. He leapt back, grabbing at his groin in agony.

"We need to get you to a hospital." I was pulling the black velvet trousers back on. They did fit. Quite well, in fact.

"I'm fine," he winced. "No need to panic. I just need a drink. Need to get my head straight." His trousers were back on.

"Are you insane? You're bleeding."

He didn't hear me, or wasn't listening, or both.

Next thing he had let himself out and was gone. I had no time to ask for the keys back.

I tried to busy myself around the house, to forget about him, the Dutch lesbian, the debacle of a week. Three hours later I Googled *fractured penis*.

According to Wikipedia, "*Penile fracture is a rupture of one or both of the tunica albuginea, the fibrous coverings that envelop the penis's corpora cavernosa. It is caused by rapid blunt force to an erect penis, usually during vaginal intercourse or aggressive masturbation … It sometimes also involves partial or complete rupture of the urethra or injury to the dorsal nerves, veins and arteries."*

It sounded damn serious. I read on: *"A popping or cracking sound, significant pain, immediate flaccidity, and skin hematoma of various sizes are commonly associated with the event."*

Then I read the part that sent me into a panicked tizz: *"Penile fracture is a medical emergency, and emergency surgical repair is the usual treatment. Delay in seeking treatment increases the complication rate. Non-surgical approaches result in 10–50% complication rates including erectile dysfunction, permanent penile curvature, damage to the urethra and pain during sexual intercourse."*

He needed to get to the hospital – like, three hours ago. Even though I hated him, even though he had well and truly busted my heart, even though I had made a vow never to go near that stupid dick of his again, I still could see he needed a doctor quick.

When I called him I could hear he was in a pub. He could barely talk from the slur.

"You need to get treatment. I've been reading … What you have is a medical emergency," I screamed.

It was pointless – there was too much noise in the background.

"I said 'YOU HAVE A MEDICAL EMERGENCY!'"

The phone went dead.

* * *

It was 7 am the following morning before he agreed to meet me at Casualty. That's 16 hours after the fracture. Within minutes of seeing a doctor he was booked in for an emergency op to have the inside of his dick sewn up. I left the doctor to do his thing. I did not want to be there helping the man who had hurt me so badly to fix the thing that had hurt me even more.

Secretly, though, I marvelled at universal pay back.

That was Sunday morning. By Monday my life had seriously spun off the rails. By Tuesday I had booked into the Hotel Hospital.

CHAPTER 8

Bipolar Suzy

The nurses' station on the second floor was all but deserted when I hauled my two suitcases and three tote bags up the stairs. It would become a familiar place, where I would have my blood pressure checked twice daily and my medication dispensed. A large white board with patients' names – and the psychiatrists and psychologists to whom they had been allocated – dominated the back wall.

I had been admitted to the General Unit, which catered for people who were suffering some sort of mental meltdown. I was given a pink bracelet, weighed and asked about allergies. I would later discover that the Generals were the privileged ones, "the ones to be". We were allowed to keep our cellphones, have visitors and go out a few hours a week, as well as on weekends. The green bracelets were the DDU (Dual Diagnosis Unit) patients who were banned from any communication with the Generals. Admitted due to substance-abuse problems coupled with some type of mood disorder, they were pretty much restricted from communication on all levels: no cellphones and no visitors for the first week.

The Eating Disorders had red wristbands and were totally isolated, on the second floor, from the Generals and Dual Diagnoses who lived side by silent side on the first. The EDs were mostly stick-thin adolescent-looking girls, all with the same walking-dead, sunken-eye, hollow look about them. The trollies of food that were wheeled about upstairs from us always carried plates covered in cling wrap, which usually consisted of three cherry tomatoes, two rice cakes and a square of yellow cheese roughly the size of a R5 coin. They received no discount on their R70 000 bill.

I was weighed and told that this was the last time I would get on a scale for the duration of my stay. Although I had managed to convince Genie in Admissions that I was not here for an eating disorder, I had told her about my binge-and-purge episodes and so she had decided to place certain restrictions on me.

The room was pleasant enough: two single beds on opposite sides and an adjoining bathroom with a shower and loo. Nurse Dirty Diana, who had huge eyes and an uncanny resemblance to the king of pop, Michael Jackson, informed me I was sharing with a girl called Babushka who was currently somewhere downstairs in the art therapy room. Nurse DD had also been assigned to go through every object I had brought in in my bags and suitcases to make sure I wasn't smuggling contraband into the clinic. As we went through each of the items in my bag, I began to tell her the story of my life. She became so entranced that she hardly noticed that I still had a pair of tweezers tucked away in my make-up bag. And when her eyes fixed on a copy of my book, *Smacked*, she became even more engaged. I decided to give her the copy, and she was thrilled. We sang a few lines of "Dirty Diana" as she moonwalked away, clutching my book. For the rest of my stay I would often catch her grabbing a quick read, in between her duties at the nurses' station. She became my greatest ally.

My first sessions with my psychiatrist and shrink were scheduled for later that afternoon, so I decided to try to nap for a few hours before lunch. It wasn't long, though, before I woke to hear someone knocking about in the room. From half-asleep, gunked-up eyes I saw the blur of a round, overweight blob of a something sitting cross-legged on the bed. It slowly dawned on me it was a girl. She looked like a ball of beige wool. Within minutes of introducing herself as Babushka, she unlocked her cupboard and asked if I was interested in seeing her catalogue. Before I could answer, a glossy array of sex toys splashed across a double-page spread was flashed before my eyes.

"This strawberry lube is the best. I have a sample here. D'you like giving blowjobs?"

Lunch was a slow sludge of floury macaroni cheese, and jelly and custard for dessert. They were not kidding about this place being a hospital. I sat on my own, watching the groups of laughing patients bond. Beneath my chatty veneer, I never realised how socially damn inadequate I had become. I plugged in my earphones, listened to Gotye's "Somebody that I Used to Know" on loop, thought about how much I hated Ex-Boyfriend, and tried to look as if I didn't care about being The Only Girl Left Alone at Lunch.

After returning my plate to the serving station, I found my way to the psychiatric section and waited to be called in for my 2 pm appointment. A tall, perfectly pressed man (who I would soon christen Dr Range Rover, after eyeing his monster multimillion-rand set of wheels) sat at an expensive-looking walnut desk. His office was über-décor trendy, with touches of high Art Deco styling. A painting by Tretchikoff hung on the wall behind him. If I squinted a little it almost looked like the woman in the picture was growing out of his head.

He took out a file and began to pummel me with a list of questions:

1. *Were there times in my life, especially when I was stressed, when I showed signs of increased talkativeness?* Tick.
2. *Did I have a decreased need for sleep?* Tick.

I began to cry at the second question and didn't stop until the end of the session.

3. *Did my thoughts often race uncontrollably?* Tick.
4. *Was I easily distracted?* Tick.
5. *Did I experience overactivity, especially in goal-directed areas?* Tick.

He went on to ask me about my sexual history. I told him about my promiscuous years at university and the spate of meaningless fucking I experienced while my mother was dying. Then I told him about my super-active sex life with Ex-Boyfriend.

He asked me about any risky adrenaline-fuelled behaviour. I spoke about my journey into drugs, my moving to Hillbrow, hanging out with whores and dealers. About not sleeping for 10 days at a time, about the lust for the crack pipe and my lungs bleeding. By the time I got to the day that I was gang raped by three dodgy criminals, he glanced up at the clock so I quickly skipped ahead to the Ferrari.

He wrote a lot down. I'm sure there were many ticks – ticks all over the place.

"Have you ever been diagnosed as Bipolar?"

Bipolar? What the fuck? Bipolar was for crazy people, loony-binners, right?

No, but I once wrote a song called "Bipolar Suzy".

I'm not sure if I thought that or said it out loud but, either way, he ignored it, closed his file and stared straight through me.

"You're showing all the signs of Bipolar 2. I would like you to attend a lecture at 3 pm – it unpacks what this disorder entails. I think you may find it interesting."

The tears were now pouring unabated from my eyes. I had been with this man for all of 20 minutes and, like some black sheep at the slaughterhouse, I had already been labelled.

He opened my file again, and wrote more.

"I want you to have a blood test first thing tomorrow. We also need to check your thyroid. I'm thinking of starting you off on a high dose of Epilim coupled with Epitec, which I'll increase slowly while we watch how your liver absorbs it. Then, for your sleep, we can start you on 200 milligrams of Seroquel."

What the fuck? Seroquel, Epitec, Epilim – what were these things?

By the time I left his office, I was devastated. I had placed so much importance on being really clean and sober since I came into recovery. I had never gone the route of psychiatric meds, ever. I had looked at all the pill poppers around me over the years, in and out of NA, and had vowed never to be like them, priding myself for really meaning I was clean when I called clean time.

I didn't want to be crazy, I didn't want some god-awful *diagnosis* and I definitely didn't want to start getting scripts, being medicated and taking pills like a fucking sheep on drugs.

I wanted to turn around and bash back into his pastel, sorbet-green office, jump up and down on his desk and shout: "I am *not* insane! Can't you see? My heart is broken. I have PTSD from a Ferrari accident. I nearly lost my job and had to pay R650 000! I found my ex in bed with a Dutch lesbian even though we had been shagging two days before! I've been writing a book on a killer athlete and I haven't slept for a year! Is that not enough reason for me to be showing symptoms of some kind of break down? Why the fuck is it so hard to just treat me for all that instead of turning me into a prescription queen, a catchment cunt for a handful of pills?"

But I was too broken to resist, never mind do the Shakira shaky-shake on his desk. I dropped my file off at the nurses' station and decided to lie down for 20 minutes before the Bipolar lecture.

Thankfully, Ms Blobby Blowjob wasn't there. I could not deal with any more talk of lubes, rabbits and vibrating eggs.

At 3 pm I found my way to the lecture room where a doctor was about to start his talk on Bipolar Disorder. Apart from a few words to Blowjob Babushka, I still hadn't actually spoken to any of my fellow inmates yet, and pretty much kept to myself. So I pretended I was at some international mental health conference and began to act like I was taking important notes on my iPad. As I tapped away on the screen, the doctor proceeded to tell us that Bipolar 2 was difficult to diagnose and for many years a lot of people had been either misdiagnosed or had been completely ignored and had been living with the disease without treatment.

He explained that more often than not a large part of the Bipolar 2's behaviour was mistaken for high-functioning behaviour or simply attributed to personality, and that a lot of Bipolar 2 patients were not aware of their hypomanic symptoms. As a result, many never sought medical help or, if they did, they were often unable to provide their doctor with all the information needed for an accurate assessment. Patients usually only sought help when they were in a depressed state.

The doctor then went to the large white board at the window and began writing.

What Are the Symptoms of Bipolar 2 Disorder?
He wrote *HYPOMANIA*.

He then went on to explain how, during a hypomanic episode, an elevated mood could show itself as either euphoric (feeling "high") or as highly irritable.

He bullet-pointed symptoms of a hypomanic episode:

- *Flying suddenly from one idea to the next.*
- *Rapid, urgent, often loud speech.*
- *Increased energy, with hyperactivity.*
- *A decreased need for sleep.*

I was trying my best to stay open-minded. Yes, I related to all four points – especially the less sleep part and the flying from one idea to the other – but I still didn't want a fucking label unless it spelt Manolo Blahnik. For a second, I smiled to myself and thought of the pair Ex-Boyfriend had bought me in London. I wondered if his dick was fixed yet.

I tuned back to the doctor at the white board who was explaining how people experiencing hypomanic episodes were often quite pleasant to be around. In fact, he said, they were often considered the life and soul of the party. They generally had a great sense of humour, were jokers and highly sociable, taking an intense interest in activities, and infecting others with their positive mood and energy.

Hmmmm … This was starting to sound scarily familiar.

"So what's so bad about all this, you may ask?" said the doctor. "Well, the problem is that hypomania can also lead to erratic and highly risky, unhealthy behaviour. Hypomanic episodes can sometimes progress to full mania, which affects a person's ability to function. In manic episodes, they might spend money they don't have – gamblers, for instance, are especially prone to this. They often seek out sex with people they normally wouldn't give a second glance, and often engage in unsafe sex, endangering their lives and other people's lives too. They might also engage in other impulsive or risky behaviours, with the potential for dangerous consequences."

I would later also read of the recent trend of Bipolar over-diagnosis. It appeared that more people than ever were being labelled with it. Even more worrying was that in the last 10 years there had been a 40 per cent increase in the number of children diagnosed with Bipolar Disorder. It also appeared that medical aid and financial institutions were more willing to reimburse a Bipolar 2 code than a "softer" diagnosis such as straight depression, for instance.

By the end of the one-hour session, I was terrified that I was indeed one of those who had slipped under the radar of diagnosis. That evening I went like a sheep to the dip, took my little cup with my pills and swallowed them like a good girl. And slept for eight hours that night. In fact, it took both a nurse and Babushka to shake me out of my Seroquel coma. For the rest of the morning I felt like I had concussion, like someone had chucked a clod of lead at my head.

In the afternoon, after a strange stir-fry lunch that could have been made with chicken or cat – I'm not sure any of us would have known the difference – I felt a terrible tiredness sweep over me. I nodded off during the lecture on Dual Diagnosis, then decided to creep into my little single bed for an hour or two, and skip dinner – served at 5 pm – in the hope of shutting myself off from the world until the night meds were ready to be handed out. It's amazing how quickly my mind was longing for a pill-induced Seroquel coma.

When I awoke it was already dark and a heavy hangover of disorientation chloroformed me. I heard a sniffing sob from across the room. Babushka sat on the bed, cross-legged. I'm not sure how long she had been there, but as she saw me wake, she switched on the lights and lurched into a tearful litany of rage against her mother and her boyfriend, both of whom appeared to have let her down by not coming to visit that evening.

I watched her jowls moving as her voice got more strident and anger spat from her pudgy lips. After 10 minutes of her non-stop yowling, I got up to fetch my laptop, a pair of earphones and a USB with three seasons of *The Walking Dead* from my padlocked cupboard.

"Sorry to interrupt," I said. Of course I wasn't. Sorry. More like fucking desperate to cut her off. "I'm afraid I really can't listen to any more of your story. I came here to recover, I came here for me. I am not your therapist, so I can't help you. Please forgive me, but right now I need to put on my earphones and watch my series."

Phew. That wasn't as hard as I thought it would be. I turned my back and started watching the zombies tear each other's limbs apart.

When I woke in the morning Babushka had moved out. For the duration of my stay, she never said another word to me. The luxury of my much-longed-for solitary room was short lived though. By 3 pm a new inmate had been allocated. This one really did look like she had walked off the set with Rick Grimes and his crew. Forget *The Walking Dead*. Cassandra barely had a pulse.

Zombie Land

For the first two days I didn't get to hear Cassandra speak. She had come in heavily medicated and semi-suicidal, and pretty much stayed blotto as they kept her knocked out. In the beginning I crept around the room so as not to wake her, but I soon discovered that she was in such a deep coma that a pharmaceuticals factory could have collapsed and she would have slept right through it.

It soon became clear that most patients who inhabited the clinic space were firing on barely one cylinder and remained in some kind of drug-induced flat-lined state. Many came in that way, already having been slaves to a cocktail of pharmaceuticals for most of their adult lives. I guess the best way for society to control people is to pump them with enough chemicals that they pose as little risk as possible.

Sure, there are those who are chemically unbalanced, who need stabilising or firing up, but with the prevalence of highly toxic foods and the debilitating and sedentary lifestyle of so many, who knows how these factors contribute to barely functioning bodies or sad and broken mindsets.

The longer I observed how we – myself and my fellow inmates – became more zombified as we responded to increasing doses of medication, the more I began to believe that the damage pharmaceuticals do to a person's soul and mind probably far outweigh the benefits. But try tell that to those who have grown to identify with their diagnosis and believe that medication is the only reason that they "function".

One thing that was achingly clear was that there were a lot of sad and lost people in this clinic. But none sadder than Clinic Boy, otherwise known as The Saddest Boy in the World, who walked into the General Unit on Day 3. The first thing I noticed were his deep green, empty eyes, which looked as though they had just cried a bucket. As I moved in closer, towards the tea area where he was stirring sugar into a cup, I could almost smell the saline on his tear-drenched black-and-red anarchy T-shirt.

Somehow, I found my voice from deep within my inner web of anxiety.

"Hi. What you in here for?" As in prison, this was the standard first-liner.

As soon as the words were out, I could sense how absofuckinglutely inappropriately dumb they were.

Clinic Boy's sad, green-glassy eyes stared right through me. From close up, I noticed he had a tinge of ginger in his unruly hair and, although he was a bit pudgy around the middle, he had a great set of calves. He was by far the hottest guy in the joint. But then, of course, we weren't exactly dealing with *GQ*'s Sexiest Man of the Year shortlist.

As soon as my words were out, I felt him ricochet, anxiety propelling him backwards. He muttered something, grabbed his tea and moved away. I would later discover that he was in for trying to kill himself, swallowing a handful of pills in an attempt to snuff himself out.

So much for my attempt at making a clinic connection. When had I become so socially inept? I used to find it so easy to make small talk, to create friendships.

I left the dining area and headed for the nurses' station where they watched me as I swallowed my evening meds. It's amazing how quickly I had become a compliant pill popper. I calculated ahead. The Seroquel would only take about 45 minutes to kick in. So I quickly headed straight for my bed to watch *The Walking*

Dead. I was still on Episode 1 of Season 1. Each time I watched I would fall asleep halfway through and then have to start watching all over again. I think I may have watched Episode 1 for 10 days. Cassandra was already in zombie land.

At breakfast the next day, unable to bear my self-imposed solitary confinement any longer, I decided to make an effort and sat down at The Black Girls' table. It's strange how, after more than 20 years into democracy, people still seemed to gravitate into racial pockets. For the first time since I'd been away, I felt at home – as at home as one can be in a place like this, I suppose. I felt at ease, a place where I could chill with a group of strangers. For a moment it felt like I was back with my magazine sisters at The Machine. The group, which became pretty fluid over the next 20 days as people came and went, would become my mealtime companions for the remainder of my stay.

As I headed off for my daily therapy session, I noticed that Babushka, the sex-toy roomie, had made a beeline for Clinic Boy and had all but kidnapped him. As I passed their table I felt her angry piggy eyes burn into me. I could only imagine the diatribe of vile she was spewing against me to the boy on whom I had a near-as-dammit crush. I wondered if she'd offered him a strawberry-lubed blowjob yet.

My therapist, Tine, was a robust, homely looking woman who immediately keyed into the idea that beyond the trauma of The Crash, the sleeplessness and the work addiction, my relationship was really what had sent me over the edge. She soon decided that what would most endanger my recovery was getting out of the clinic and gravitating back to Ex-Boyfriend.

And then, five days after I booked in, he arrived entirely unexpectedly with a carefully prepared baked vegetarian lasagne and a tiny green stone, which he told me to wear close to my heart because it would help me to find clarity and unravel the truth. The truth was I hated him for arriving in my space without warning; I hated him seeing me so small and raw and vulnerable. And I really hated this food he had brought along to placate, patronise and control me. When he finally left I dumped the untouched lasagne into the bin and cried my eyes out in my room. The day after, Tine could clearly see how upset I was, but it gave us some good stuff to work with. There was no denying that this person still had a huge effect on me.

The more therapy sessions I shared with Tine, the more I came to realise how I needed to deal with the often all-consuming feelings that were eating into my brain, my soul, my bones, the craziness that came directly as a result of my toxic relationship. The big question of how I was going to get over him preoccupied most of our sessions.

I found the concept a strange one. How do you "get over" someone? Do you take a good run up and, from a distance, leap over the person you are trying to forget, like a hurdles race you see on telly during the Olympics? Do they go away then? And once you've made the jump, what do you do with the body and the memories? Are they simply erased as you make that leap? Do you hang him on the line in some far-off, desolated space and hope the crows wheeling overhead will get at him, peck his eyes out, hack the flesh from between his shoulders, and tear him up into tiny ribbons of flesh fluttering in the wind?

Until Tine I had only ever been to male therapists, so having a woman to speak to was an entirely new and enlightening experience. I used none of my old manipulative flirt-with-the-doctor tricks and found myself "honesting up" much quicker with her. Plus, I guess I knew I had limited time on this R70 000 three-week sojourn, and what I most wanted was to leave in some way recovered, or at least closer to being the me I was longing to find. So I really trusted her when she told me that staying away from Ex-Boyfriend would be key to me getting stronger.

By the end of our first week of sessions together, she ignited one of those *aha!*, life-expanding moments when she got me to realise what an acute connection there was between Ex-Boyfriend and my mother. The problematic drinking, the extreme judgmentalism, the heartlessness, harshness, the inability to apologise, the lack of emotional intimacy, the critical parent – I had never been aware of how the two resembled each other.

By way of Tine, I soon came to see that the way I had behaved around my mom was identical to the way I behaved around Ex-Boyfriend: always trying to impress, perform, achieve, to love them more and love them better, the never-ending cycle of slaving to get their love and attention. But their approval had always remained just out of reach. The never-ending criticism that would keep me on the hamster wheel, the voice that was always saying, "Try harder – you still haven't impressed me". That same big-black-hole feeling I would get whenever I got too near to or too far away from them. That sinking feeling that would envelop everything when I felt I had disappointed them. And me falling deeper and deeper into a ravine, trying to dance harder and harder to make them love me ... But finding nothing but the darkness.

And, of course, that stale stench of wine.

The other biggie was the whole food issue. Both my mother and Ex-Boyfriend cooked for me, prepared meals that were packed with layers and layers of "stuff", layers of manipulation spiced with resentments. Food was never simply made with love. And once the meal was gone, consumed, and the plate was empty, a sense of feeling over-satiated – overfull – would engulf me, which would in turn send me straight to the lavatory, head in the toilet bowl, to purge all of it. Ridding myself of all the toxicity was my pathetic attempt to control all the crazy, hollow feelings that emerged just by being near them.

As I spoke to Tine, it became clear how confused I had become by the idea of love and care. And how, in fact, that which I thought was nurturing me was actually throttling, even killing me. When I finally leapt into this place of clarity, I got to embrace my Plathian moment – the moment I realised that, in order to get better, I would need to kill both of them, with one really well-aimed stone.

CHAPTER 10

Narcissist Victim Syndrome

It was in one of my many therapy sessions at the clinic that I first came across the term "Narcissist Victim Syndrome".

Up until the time I booked into the Hotel Hospital, I had made many assumptions about myself, based on accusations where both Ex-Boyfriend and my mother, during my childhood, had accused me of being a selfish, thoughtless, self-consumed narcissist. I had heard it so often, especially during the transition into adolescence, when I became a teenager and my mother had become increasingly affronted by any trait I displayed that threatened her domain over me. If ever I expressed a thought or action different to hers, I was accused of disobedience, selfishness and betrayal. As a result, my rebel self exploded and I went off the rails in order to resist her.

A deep schism ripped our once-close relationship apart and I embarked on a crazy self-destructive journey to counteract her influence on me, finally finding myself lost in the clutches of extreme heroin and crack addiction, homeless, and close to the brink of death. In hindsight I was actually impressed that I had had the courage to resist what I saw now as clearly narcissistic ploys.

But by the time I embarked on my relationship with Ex-Boyfriend, I had far less ability to discern – perhaps because I was a lot more worn down. Whenever I threw myself passionately into a project or got too independent of him, accusations would follow of how selfish or in love with myself I was. In my defence, I never gave up a project or activity just to please him, but instead of telling him to fuck right off, I wasted far too much time trying to placate him and dim my own shine. I often found myself stopping short of telling him of my successes or dreams lest I upset him. It was the classic case of tiptoeing on eggshells whenever I thought I may dent his fragile ego.

About two weeks into my stay at Hotel Hospital, we had a lecture on NPD – Narcissistic Personality Disorder – at which point I heard for the first time the Greek legend of Narcissus and his sidekick Echo. I found it intriguing and during the 90-minute session I had many light-bulb moments.

Essentially, the story goes something like this …

One day a beautiful young nymph, Echo, spots the gorgeous 16-year-old Narcissus as he is out hunting deer. Echo's greatest character defect is that she talks too much. When Echo prevents Hera from busting her husband Zeus for cheating on her, because she has been distracted by Echo's mindless chatter, Hera punishes Echo by taking away her voice so that she is only able to repeat whatever she hears. Echo … echo … echo.

Echo, of course, falls in love with Narcissus but Hera's curse means that she's unable to say anything original. She follows him around a lot and when, one day, he inadvertently says, "Let's get together," she runs after him, thinking he has finally succumbed to her love.

But instead of reciprocating, he rejects her. Harshly.

Highly distraught, Echo hides in a cave. She gets skinnier and skinnier, as she slowly pines away, until her flesh literally becomes dust. Finally, her bones turn to stone, and all that remains is her echoing voice.

Meanwhile, Narcissus runs around meeting and rejecting chicks – as all good narcissists do, of course. No one is good enough for him. One day he stops for a drink at a small pond. When he sees his own reflection in the water of the pool, he falls hopelessly in love – with himself. As he tries to touch the image he has fallen for, the water dissipates and the image disperses. Unable to capture his reflection, Narcissus stays by the pond until he starves to death.

The moral of the story is used as a warning to avoid loving a person who cannot love you back because they are too taken with themselves.

As I sat in the lecture and listened, everything about this story resonated deep within. I was transfixed. I took my thoughts to therapy later, where Tine and I began to really work on my new realisation that I had been with at least two strong narcissists in my life.

Beyond my sessions with Tine, I went on an all-out Google mission to research and read as much as I could on Narcissist Victim Syndrome and soon came across a list of symptoms that a *victim* of a narcissist often displayed. They were, in fact, very similar to those of the post-traumatic stress I had suffered as a result of The Crash. For instance, just as I had experienced flashbacks about the Ferrari, so too did I constantly suffer recollections of past traumatic incidences with Ex-Boyfriend. Then there were the bouts of high irritability and outbursts of anger. I was also often plagued by depression, and suffered enormously from a lot of unfounded guilt. There was, too, a general feeling of numbness, and impaired concentration and memory. Of course, sleep was often elusive and disturbed, occasionally peppered with distressing dreams.

When I found a list of traits of a Narcissistic Mother, not only did I see many that my own mother displayed, but there were a number that I recognised in myself, which I had developed while raising my two boys.

- Self-absorbed. The Narcissist Mother's feelings and desires are much more important than yours.
- Extremely sensitive to criticism.
- Irrationally defensive.

- Incredibly angry, and that anger is used to manipulate her children to adhere to her wishes.
- Childish and petty. Getting even with you is a constant.
- She hands over parental responsibilities as soon as she can.
- In her world, she is always right and never apologises about anything.
- She is devoid of empathy for you or others.

I began to have a rush of memories of how I had tried so hard to rescue my narcissist mom when I was a child, staring at the phone in the entrance hall, trying to find the courage to dial Alcoholics Anonymous whose number I had found in the classified section of *The Star* newspaper. I sincerely believed that if I managed to make that call they would come to our house, pick up my inebriated mommy and rescue all of us. I hated myself for not being able to dial, to save my mother's life. At that age I had not yet internalised the concept of powerlessness, and yet I remained intrinsically dumbstruck and shattered by my own. And so the self-hatred began, my life's journey pointing in the direction of a town called Self-Destruction.

My shrink explained how many children from dysfunctional narcissistic family systems or any type of abusive relationship often see themselves as the ones at fault, who believe that *they* are the narcissists.

"Your mother probably groomed you to always blame yourself as a way of forcing you not to be able to look at her and question her," she explained. "And it was probably the same story when it came to your boyfriend."

Oh yes, for sure it was and, when it came to Ex-Boyfriend, I spent even more time and energy interrogating myself about all my faults. Like my mother, he ticked a whole lot of the NPD boxes:

- Grandiose to the extreme, priding himself as being one of a kind, and overly self-important in a world he has constructed.
- In the beginning, he is charming, attractive and attentive. He is romantic, cooks dinners and is highly sexually competent. (Actually, highly sexually competent was the one constant throughout our relationship.)

- He believes that other people (especially me) will never be able to survive without him.
- He disregards or diminishes everyone else's feelings.
- He can never accept his own inadequacies, and believes others are always at fault.
- He often comes up with grand, exciting plans – but rarely follows through with them.
- His lack of empathy for the world can taint everything.

Although there were many times during our relationship when I could clearly see that he was a chauvinist narcissist and that his behaviour was often entirely unacceptable – I knew most of my friends thought as much – my Echo system was so strong that before I could even properly formulate a critical thought, I would slip into excusing all his behaviour, telling myself that all he needed was a bit of love.

He was adopted, I kept reminding myself; he had been through untold hell and misery throughout his childhood, which made him feel unwanted. I felt the hole in his soul and perhaps, if I just tried a little harder, worked on myself a bit more, was less selfish and more forgiving, surely I could love him well again and his narcissism would be cured and we could live the rest of our lives happily ever after …

So I stuck by him regardless of what the signs were telling me.

And that's why that blow, when he finally pulled the plug on me, hit me so hard, deep in the solar plexus. *Because I was the one who was meant to leave him.* All logic told me that. The fact was that when he finally left I never saw it coming, not even for a second, because I had been so busy "sticking it out with him".

Finally, as Tine explained how a narcissist tends to initiate his own abandonment because he is so terrified of being left himself, things began to make sense to me. He would far rather control the loss of a relationship than ever be a victim of hurt or abandonment. His greatest fear is emotional pain and he is so terrified of losing his sources of Narcissistic Supply (and of being emotionally hurt) that it feels only right that he should be the one calling "game over".

In fact, as I began to do the work of looking back, I saw how Ex-Boyfriend had actually made it a goal, from early on, to end the relationship, another bullet point on his "to do" list. I think even he was shocked at having allowed it to go on for as long as he did. I remember sometimes asking, "How long do you think we'll be together?", hoping he'd be able to see the same happily-ever-after scenario I had playing in my head. Then he'd pretend to look at his wristwatch and say, "Another five minutes, babe." I used to laugh at his sense of humour. Problem was, he wasn't joking.

So, with all this newfound information, and in the safe confines of therapy, it became blatantly clear to me that I needed to move on. And, in my usual way of doing things, I immediately wanted to demonise him, burn all evidence of him and get over him. Tine had to remind me that I was embarking on a process, not a decision or an event.

She made me do a lot of written work around him and our relationship in order to acknowledge and accept the painful reality I had endured, being involved with both him and my mother. Just as I had done in the early stages of my drug recovery, writing pages and pages around the unmanageability of my life due to drugs and my inability to control my using, so too did I need to put in the written work around my two departed narcissists, to whom in different ways I had also been addicted.

Becoming self-aware and seeing my own complicit role were vital in order for me to digest the full extent of the toxic nature of these relationships. Slowly I began to accept how truly destructive both had been for me, and no matter how great the sex was with Ex-Boyfriend, it would never be able to erase all the glaring problems that tainted everything else.

But if I thought I had cried many tears before I arrived at the clinic, I was shocked by how many more I still needed to shed in my grieving. I cried for many reasons, but I think my tears really bled for me, for the abuse and betrayal I had allowed myself to go through. I had to accept responsibility for that. No one had forced me to stay.

So what really cut me deeply is: why had I thought so little of myself that I had believed I had deserved this situation? And ... would I ever be able to trust myself, and have the courage to love again?

CHAPTER 11

Clinic Boy

When I connected with Clinic Boy in the last few days of my stay at Hotel Hospital, I felt like I had come face to face with my soul match, as twee as that may sound. That he was 12 years younger than me, drifting from one handyman job to another, living in a cottage on his parents' property and regularly fighting off suicidal urges were of very little consequence to me. All I saw was a beautiful, sensitive soul.

Of course both my therapist and psychiatrist were horrified by the idea of a new attraction, especially one that had originated in the clinic, but I was deaf to all reason. It felt like the universe had smiled down on me and afforded me redemption from all the pain I had endured at the hands of Ex-Boyfriend.

Plus, whenever I was in the proximity of Clinic Boy, I felt healed, like I was a new person. In fact, it wasn't just around Clinic Boy that I was experiencing this re-ignition of ideas and realisations. In the Hotel Hospital I had begun to feel like some kind of change agent around any number of people. Even my roommate Cassandra had sprung to life, pitching up for breakfast on time, hair neatly combed and a slick of red lipstick brightening her once-pallid face. And if Little Miss Walking Dead could be revived, then anything was possible.

After Babushka left the clinic in a storm of sniffles and tears, Clinic Boy and I slowly began exchanging looks and little interchanges out in the sunshine where the smokers gathered for puffs between classes. He always had a swarm of at least five chicks around him so I tended to hang back, me being all lion and proud, not ever wanting to give the impression that I liked, never mind *needed*, his attention. But nevertheless a connection was growing.

Two days before I left we touched for the first time. Well, it wasn't intentional really. We were in a class, learning about something called Imago relationship therapy, and in the shuffle for seats, we found ourselves next to each other. From the description on the board, it sounded exactly like the stuff I needed to hear.

In that class I found out that Imago, from the Latin for "image", is regarded as a highly effective form of relationship and couples transformational therapy, developed 25 years ago by American therapists Dr Harville Hendrix and Dr Helen LaKelly Hunt. During the lecture I came to understand that the particular image we have of love will ultimately influence the way someone will love us when we embark on a love relationship. Essentially, as human beings, we understand what love is from the way our parents and other significant adults have loved us and, conversely, how we have loved them. So, the lecturer explained, it's really all about being fully aware of our parental love, because that primary bond will have huge significance on how we later behave when we are "in love".

My mind was on fire. I found the entire concept fascinating and many truth bells began ringing in that session. I found it almost creepy how this so precisely reflected my relationships with both the alcoholic Ex-Boyfriend and my deceased mother. I found it especially fascinating that we are attracted to someone who exhibits parts of ourselves that haven't yet been developed, parts we may never have been allowed to express. When we meet someone who fulfils this, they may feel strangely familiar to us – hence the feeling of a meeting of souls – but what is really happening is that we're being attracted to someone because of needs that remain unmet in parental or caregiver relationships.

Wow. This blew my mind. Why the fuck would I want to meet a man who reminded me of my dead, elusive father or of my emotionally unavailable, often cruel mother? And yet the lecturer emphasised that this was unavoidable until we worked through these parts of ourselves – that those relationships were there to allow us to be whole and healthy within ourselves.

Then he dropped another bombshell. "Some of the things you love in the beginning about your partner you will hate and resent later! In fact, the very things you were initially attracted by will, in time, become a source of conflict later. If you thought your partner was free-spirited and playful in the beginning, you will find them irresponsible and thoughtless later. What you first saw as being highly attractive, ambitious and stable will later become rigid and boring."

This stuff was insanely scary!

"So will no one ever be able to sustain the initial allure?" I asked the lecturer, glancing furtively at Clinic Boy beside me. Surely I would always love his gentle quietness, his soft faraway eyes.

"Once the pheromones fade, that initial allure will change to something else," the lecturer explained. "But this is where conflict comes in – and conflict, of course, is just another word for healing and growth trying to take place. Conflict is necessary for something new to be born. It is the window to deeper intimacy. In fact, there is no such thing as an incompatible relationship. If your partner doesn't fulfil your needs, it's just an opportunity for you to look within and work on filling the hole within yourself."

Gooseflesh rippled across my skin, a tingle down my back.

It was all so intriguing that I hardly noticed my arm touching that of Clinic Boy, who seemed just as enraptured as I was. (In truth, it was just the fine hairs on our forearms that lightly stroked each other, but sitting in the room, with our chairs leaning against walls, kissed by the dying sun, it felt like an electric chemical storm.)

That night we WhatsApped each other from the north and south wings of the clinic. It was incredible what a deep and intense connection had suddenly developed. The conversation got sexual pretty quickly, and I should have wondered there and then what that was all about … And yet, it felt completely normal at the time.

Sex was always an easy place for me to go to. "You really need to look at that stuff," Tine warned during our last official clinic session. "Why you find it so easy to go there." But I was enjoying the flood of feel-good chemicals in my brain every time I thought of the messages from Clinic Boy. However, I did begrudgingly set up another appointment to see her the following week.

When I finally left, I said goodbye to very few people. I am not good with endings. But just before I drove off, I made sure that I found Clinic Boy. I had retrieved a copy of *Smacked* from home on a day pass and I wrote him a special note and gave him the book of my heart and my life. It felt like I was giving him the key to my soul.

The following night I went back to the clinic to attend an NA meeting but, if truth be told, it really was to catch a bit of time with Clinic Boy. I made great effort to look good: snakeskin skirt, purple knitted top, Patrick Cox London leather shoes.

He was outside with a visitor when I arrived, so I made my way to the back section, where patients smoke, and that's where I saw Pregnant Girl.

"Isn't it amazing how people have fallen in love with each other here?" she beamed. I was about to ask her how she knew about me and Clinic Boy when I realised that she wasn't talking about us. Her eyes gleamed as she gushed about how she had fallen for a young dude called Blake and that "Suanne and Ryan [yes, Clinic Boy] are now an item too".

I was stunned. Crushed. I saw only a blur of faces in front of me. I muttered some excuse and hot-footed it to where Clinic Boy and his friend were still smoking. Without thinking twice, I spat through pursed lips that I needed to speak to him. Urgently. Without another word, I hauled him off, pulled him into the lift and pushed the Up and Down buttons so no one could interrupt us. I demanded an explanation. After all the betrayals of Ex-Boyfriend, my feelers for being fucked over were on super high alert.

"Are you fucking with my head? Are you seeing that airhead Suanne? I need you to be straight with me – what the fuck is going on?"

Just as I got really sexual really quickly, so too could I get jealous in an instant. If only I could have seen how crazy that was – but of course I didn't. I was too busy relishing in the flood of "love" chemicals.

He looked amused, happy even. I punched the Up and Down buttons again. He assured me that there was nothing. He said it was all a misunderstanding, that Pregnant Girl was still a child and had got things wrong, blah blah blah. I wanted to – needed to – believe him and so I did. Then he took my face in his hands and smiled deeply at me. Angels began to sing.

He walked with me to the car park, his arm lightly around my shoulder. His tall, bulky frame dwarfed mine, and it felt so good, this huge comforter. Then, like a sweet boy in high school, he asked if I would go out with him on Thursday night. That was a few nights away. The day he was leaving the clinic. A band called Die Dooie Diere was playing at a little club called Amuse Café in Linden. He whispered into my ear that he would love me to meet him there. My heart flipped, skipped a thousand beats. A date. Yay. How long ago had it been since I had been asked out on a date? Even if it was to a band called The Dead Animals, I didn't care. And then he gently touched my face and his lips met mine and the sweetest, slowest kiss in the world ensued. It went on for what felt like at least three lifetimes. The dreaminess of it all accompanied me home across the city as I half-drove half-flew through the black night in Pegasus, my Pajero sport. Short-wheel base, zero to 100 in 9.2 seconds.

CHAPTER 12

Getting Out

From the very beginning, back when I first got into recovery in 1999, I had always been incredibly fastidious about being completely clean. I was highly suspicious of most pharmaceuticals because, I believed, they often suppressed symptoms instead of encouraging people to address the root cause of their affliction. I chose instead to embrace doing mountains of written step work of self-interrogation and reflection. So whenever a therapist I consulted suggested I get assessed to go on psychiatric meds, I simply stopped seeing him.

So, on the day I drove out of the boomed gate of the Hotel Hospital, I felt like a bloody drug dealer. I had a bag filled to the brim of different-coloured and -shaped pills plus a prescription for a three-month top-up. Somehow, because I had been surrounded by a lot of people who were all on some kind of medication, endorsed by a brigade of white coats who not only encouraged but insisted you needed chemicals to heal, it had become entirely natural that I should comply and become a member of the pill-popping army.

It was only months later that I got to see how desperate I must have been to have checked into the clinic, how sad and broken I had been when I had so easily bought into my diagnosis and how terrified I had become of returning to the out-of-control space I had been in before I hospitalised myself.

The thing is that any fool should have been able to see that I was traumatised when I signed on the dotted line, the one that said, "Give us 70 grand up front" prior to admission to the clinic. Finding a Dutch lesbian in your man's bed, writing off a R3.2-million Ferrari, not sleeping for a year, facing the chop at work, watching your recent Ex-Boyfriend's penis snap, plus writing a book about a stump-legged, psychotic athlete ... Well, hello! Who wouldn't feel a tad out of control?

But I had lost the ability to reason, and by the time I left I had completely bought into my Bipolar 2 diagnosis. My inability to sleep had played a large part in my compliance and once I found a way to shut my eyes again using the little white pill called Seroquel I was so grateful that I was prepared to do almost anything to avoid insomnia. Besides, Dr Range Rover reassured me, Seroquel – nicknamed "Quiet Time" by the nurses and "Sluroquel" by the patients – was not addictive.

While in the clinic, I hadn't really noticed but on getting out, and with the weekly increase of prescribed meds (as I had been instructed by Dr Range Rover), it soon became obvious that some of these chemicals, my supposed cure, had begun to change the chemicals in my brain.

The first thing I became aware of was my sleeping. Well, actually it felt a lot like dying ... I no longer woke up with the birds, before the dawn cracked the black sky like popcorn. I now needed an alarm that would traumatise me out of a dead coma. Gone were the pre-sunrise dawns when I would reach for my iPad while the world slept, when I would literally pop awake like a bud bursting, aching with a throb of creativity to write the next chapter of my new book. That had all gone. But when I voiced my concerns with Dr Range Rover, that the meds might be hampering my creativity, he pooh-poohed the idea and said that many creatives thrived on Bipolar medication. In fact, he told me, world leaders, artists and important successful business people were often Bipolar 2 and they all functioned incredibly well on meds. So who was I to argue with a learned doctor, right?

But by the time I had been out for four weeks I realised I had not written a single word. Not one. It was as if my mind had become a sluggish mishmash of papier mâché sludge.

The next issue that emerged was the forgetfulness. It felt like some kind of parasite, a two-headed *Giardia* monster, had eaten away at the short-term segment of my brain, the part that was supposed to remember where I put things.

I once found myself returning to my house five times, forgetting first my wallet, then my driver's licence, then back for the flask of coffee I had left on the kitchen counter. Halfway down the road I couldn't remember whether I had locked the front door and alarmed the house. After having driven back four times, I was almost a kilometre away when I turned back to see whether I had closed the remote-control gate. Tears streaming down my face, I began to feel like I was going insane. Only, this time, it was for real. And it was being caused by the pills that were supposed to help me, cure me.

Even cooking had become a danger, especially when any form of multitasking came into play. Before the clinic I was able to send messages, answer calls, write shopping lists, clean up and cook all at the same time. Now, if I took my mind off the activity at hand, I would forget whatever else I was doing. One night I went to great lengths to impress Clinic Boy with a rogan josh curry. While cooking I got caught up in a convo on Facebook, my iPad to the left of the stove. The next thing the curry began spattering furiously over the hot plate. Without thinking I grabbed a spoon to check if the yoghurt I had added had curdled. The bubbling rogan josh scalded my lip and tongue. Without stopping to tend my singed mouth, my mind leapt to the conclusion that the curry was missing something so I grabbed the black peppercorn shaker. Next thing, the lid fell off into the boiling red sauce and a hundred peppercorns went tumbling in. My hand flew into it, aiming to rescue the bobbing corns. And, fingers burning and yelping like a singed hen, I sunk into a scalded mess of tears.

It was as though I had lost the ability to think logically and action effectively.

But the thing that really tipped the scales for me was waking up with heart palpitations – so crippled with anxiety that I could barely leave my bed. I was plagued by dreams in which psychotic bears and snakes 10 metres long were coming after me. By this stage I had done as the prescription had ordered and had increased my dosage of Epitec to 175 milligrams and Epilim to 200 milligrams. The Seroquel dosage was now at 200 milligrams. In utter desperation I made an appointment to see the Art Deco, Thomas Pink-loving psychiatrist.

During the 30-minute session that cost R2500 an hour, Dr Range Rover grudgingly agreed that, on this particular cocktail, some people might experience some memory loss and nightmares. He seemed unable to admit, though, that perhaps the meds were doing more harm than good. That was the last time I saw Dr Range Rover.

Instead, I began to do mountains of my own reading, searching for others who may be experiencing the ill-effects of the psych meds I now seemed to be imprisoned by.

I soon found out that the white tablet Epilim was a lot more potent than its unassuming veneer first indicated. Side effects included abnormal eye movement, concentration problems, deafness, hallucinations or convulsions, potentially severe liver problems, weakness, loss of appetite, lethargy, oedema, drowsiness, jaundice, memory issues, thoughts of suicide, unexplained bruising or bleeding and even weight gain.

Weight gain? Oh my god, did I read that right? Of all the side effects, that seemed the most horrendous.

And then there was Seroquel: dry mouth, sleepiness, dizziness, body aches, weakness, vomiting, increased appetite, irritability, trouble concentrating, thinking, or speaking clearly, clumsiness, unusual dreams, loss of interest in sex, fainting, seizures, irregular heartbeat, difficulty breathing or swallowing, swelling of the face, lips, or tongue, thoughts of suicide or harming yourself, and – once again – weight gain.

Armed with these horrific facts I headed off to the psych med forums, which I soon found out resembled the Abu Ghraib of the pharma world. The Bipolar ones were some of the scariest. The stories terrified me ...

I've been diagnosed with Biopolar Disorder. My psych gave me Epitec starting with 50 mg for two weeks, and then 85mg for another two weeks, 100 mg for 42 days, and now I'm on Epitec 200 mg. I also take [Seroquel] and at night I take 300 mg mood stabiliser to help me sleep, with 25 mg Stilnox. I'm suffering with a very fast heartbeat and my chest feels tight and makes it difficult for me to breathe. I recently developed stomach ulcers and I've gained 20 kg in five months. I also feel like I have lost my memory. Can this be a sign of any side effects of Epitec and what should I do about it?

And:

Epilim is often not a nice drug for people to take. I took Epilim for 10½ years. I have very little memory of that time. It also destroyed my red blood cells, made me gain weight … I was very impatient with people. I had no life. Most of my time was spent asleep. It made me suicidal and destroyed any chance that I had of having a life, going to work or getting married and having a family. My life began when I came off Epilim.

After reading reams and reams of similar sad-ass stories, instead of increasing the dosage – as I had been advised to do by Dr RR – I now began a slow process of cutting down, first to 150 milligrams, then 120, and then 100. But I was terrified of stopping them all together. What if I reverted to that sad, mad, crazy me? What if I couldn't stop crying, and stayed awake until the world ended?

CHAPTER 13

The Unbearable Heaviness of Waiting

The morning of my first date with Clinic Boy, I cut my almost waist-length hair. It had been just under a week since I had discharged myself. For the longest time, Ex-Boyfriend had told me never to cut my hair and I had complied and worn my hair long throughout our relationship. I had a huge amount of hair and it got in the way of everything, so most of the time I would end up wearing it scrunched up and tied away, but once in a while I would visit Dee, my Eartha Kitt-voiced hairdresser, where it would be washed, treated, blown and GHDed to make it all lovely, slinky and shiny.

Ex-Boyfriend believed that within our hair lay our power – his lengthy dreads were his testament to the belief. So I decided that chopping my hair off would be a final "fuck you" to him. Plus, with this 12-year age gap looming between Clinic Boy and me, I told myself that I needed to do something to trendify my look.

The results were impressive. In my scuffed-up Zara jeans, which I'd bought on the island of Majorca on an international launch of the Toyota Corolla, my ankle-length boots, black netty

New York top and new edgy chin-length hair cut, I felt a hundred years younger.

I could hardly breathe as I parked the new Range Rover Evoque in the parking lot of Amuse Café that Thursday night. It was the only new car among a host of beaten-up old Mazda 323s and 10-year-old Polos and Audis. There was a newish Picanto and a little Auris that could have been 2013, but still mine stuck out like a concept car at a motor show.

Walking through the parking lot towards the entrance felt a bit like the Walk of Shame on *Survivor*. Even with my attempts to dress down and casual, my newly cut head of sleek-ironed hair pushed me clearly into the "you made too much effort" category.

I paid the R40 entrance to a tattooed, nose-ringed, androgynous-looking child-man and scouted the dimly lit venue for Clinic Boy. The club was half empty. Everyone was in black. Even my tattered jeans stuck out as too colourful. A half-dressed mannequin on the stage seemed to be the only other one, besides me, who had made an effort.

I spotted Clinic Boy leaning against the bar, beer in hand. I really wanted to run away or at the very least down a double whiskey, and could have easily turned away right then and leapt back into my metal steed. Instead, I forced myself towards him, my anxiety levels shooting through my frontal lobe. Was it the Epilim or the Epitec that was making me feel this way?

The moment he felt my touch and turned towards me was like one of those slow-motion movie scenes. In this place where public displays of affection were so not on, where being cool and detached was *de rigueur*, our lips met, then our tongues and, for an extended elastic moment, the world stopped, as we slowly slipped through a crack in time. It felt like a Mills & Boon novel set against a backdrop of *The Walking Dead*.

The rest of the night we spent entwined, as singer Kobus, clad in Johnny Cash black, monotonously read poems such as "Die Highways Bloei", Die Dooie Diere churning out tortured, guttural echoes in the background.

It was just after midnight when we drove in convoy to my place.

I made sure not to go zero to 100 in 6.5 seconds in my Evoque lest his little black Atos was left behind.

Unlike with Ex-Boyfriend, sex with Clinic Boy was weird. He was a world-class kisser, a champ in pussy licking, but when it came to the penetration game he seemed to lose the plot. Like a typical straight-jacketed Afrikaner boy, he opted for the missionary position and refused any deviation. He would often break off halfway through the act, ashamed by his performance, convinced I was assessing and judging him. No amount of reassurance could change his mind. Having come out of a super-confident sex-on-tap relationship, this was almost disorientating, but I convinced myself it was good for me, that it was just what I needed. This, I told myself, was exactly where the universe wished to place me.

During my weekly sessions with Tine, I would start off by painting a rosy-pink star-spangled picture of how happy I was with Clinic Boy and then leap straight into the disappointing sex, in lurid detail.

Almost all therapists advise a client not to get involved in a relationship after experiencing trauma or in the first year of recovery from an addiction. So when both Tine and Dr Range Rover suggested I abstain from the game of love, I flipped out like a demented Masha in *The Three Sisters*. "I don't have time to wait! I'm getting older with each second that passes – I don't have a whole year. I need to shift gears, move forward – I need love now!"

In hindsight, of course, they were right. I was like a raw-skinned, mewling baby and, in that achingly vulnerable state, my magnets of neediness collided full force with Clinic Boy. As our bottomless pits engulfed us, we were foils for each other.

But at the time it was impossible for me to heed their advice. During those first few post-clinic weeks, mixed with a cocktail of prescription medication, my impatience levels were off the radar. My cheeks burnt with rage every time I had to wait more than three seconds for just about anything.

Sometimes it felt like I had been waiting forever. Waiting for time to tick, waiting for a phone to ring, a robot to change, an email to be answered, the toaster to ping, the fire to light, my period to come, my child to be born, my hair to grow, the cheque to clear, the alarm to sound, the power to come on, the paint to dry – but on the scale of The Worst Waits Ever That a Woman Must Endure, waiting for a man to call must be top of the list.

Clinic Boy became the king of making me wait.

I could send him a WhatsApp on Monday and only hear from him on Wednesday. I could call him and let the phone ring into the big black bunch of wires that stretched across the world into the night sky. It would ring forever, echoing into eternity. He had no voicemail. I was sure that he was right next to the screaming machine, grinning at his phone as it rung off the hook, getting some weird kind of power surge. Knowing he was making me wait.

The waiting – that constant, nagging waiting – drove a nail into my deepest feelings of fear and abandonment. And the thing with waiting is that it's a little like the more you love, the more you love – and the more you wait, the more you wait.

The power play of waiting also resonated deeply with what's known as the Dance of the Codependent. He withdraws. She panics. He withdraws more. She panics more. Until he withdraws so far out that he just falls off the edge of the world – and still she waits.

When he put me through one of those regular interminable waits, it would take all my strength not to keep an eye on the phone for the little WhatsApp icon, or to listen for the ping of an incoming message. I would try to be spiritual and breathe and breathe and breathe and not freak the fuck out. But, try as I might, while I was sitting on my hands holding my breath, all the stuff about surrender and powerlessness I had learned in NA and AA and whatever other fucking anonymous groups I had ever attended would lie in tatters around me like a wind-shredded paper dress.

Sometimes it felt like a grinder had taken my insides and ripped me inside out. But the underlying thought that kept me hostage all through the waiting was how much of my responses and emotions were real or whether they were being determined and influenced by the head meds I had got into the habit of swallowing daily.

CHAPTER 14

Imago That

On the first weekend together, after the night of romance at Die Dooie Diere, Clinic Boy suggested that we go to Oppikoppi, South Africa's largest music festival. Although it was still three months away, it began to take on a special significance on the bucket list of things to do in our relationship. Like some kind of road trip to Mecca, it promised to either darken or lighten the way.

First established in 1994, Oppikoppi has grown over the years to become a four-day event with both local and international acts entertaining a 30 000-strong crowd of serious revellers. Debauchery and copious amounts of drugs and alcohol are the order of the day. I was both terrified and intrigued by the idea, but as the August date drew nearer, my nagging fears began to niggle and wiggle. I, however, refused to pay much attention, blocking my ears to the many, many stories that keep popping up around me about people getting trashed from morning to night, alcohol and drug-addled ravers puking into the vegetation and the loos being no-go areas, stench pools of flies and shit and vomit.

Clinic Boy's circle of friends talked constantly about how trashed they were going to get, what drugs they were going to take, who'd be bringing the magic mushrooms, the coke, the Jack Daniels, the skank. It reminded me of when I was pregnant, how people would relish in relaying horror labour tales, oblivious that these engendered such fear that if I could have pushed the reverse baby birth button, I would have.

But my desire to share in Clinic Boy's world far outweighed my terror. Considering everything I had been through over the previous year or so – and with the anniversary of The Crash on the horizon – a lot about this relationship was giving me an incredible surge of youth, reminding me of my younger self, a time of innocence and possibility, when the world was mine to leap across. I decided I needed to pull on my big-girl boots and march into the battlefields of a new and unchartered unknown.

Besides, at that point I was almost 15 years clean ... Surely a decade and a half of practice would be like having done bench presses to strengthen the soul, having honed those muscles of clarity and resistance, and given me armour against the desire to get wasted?

Now, anyone in recovery would have asked, are you fucking mad to want to go to a place like this? This is the absolute worst torture any addict could put herself through ... But I had been feeling so trapped, held hostage by my sobriety for so long, that my entire being was longing to just chill and live alongside the "normals" out there. I was tired, tired of always having to be the poster child for clean and sober, being this boring little Sobriety Girl Guide. It felt like I'd been watching the world spin by, the uninvited guest alone at the table, staring through the window, while the party goes on next door. Boo-fucking-hoo! Jeez, get a grip, chick, I told myself – I hated it when I felt sorry for myself.

And so I decided to turn the volume of the warning voices right down and focus instead on making a "what to pack for a rock festival" list. I had a clutch of motoring-industry branded rucksacks and overnight bags from which to choose. Merrell shoes, a tube of Clarens sunblock, a touch of YSL lippie, the Beats headphones I was reviewing, my snazzy iPad cigarette charger, and the cool little hoodie I got at the recent Mini Cooper launch. I settled on the Thule rucksack for luggage.

But then, the night before we were due to leave for Oppikoppi, Clinic Boy and I had a fight. Well, not a real blood-and-guts kind of fight, because it was all done on WhatsApp, but a virtual fight, the kind more and more people on our planet are having these days.

I had organised a huge Toyota FJ Cruiser for our journey. I liked to call it my mini Hummer, just a lot less obscene. Best of all, it had this bad-boy rock-star vibe, the perfect vehicle in which to thunder around in the bush at an off-road rock festival.

Clinic Boy had, in the meantime, acquired a nippy little Jimny, which was adequate enough off road, but when it comes down to the nuts and bolts it was not even in the same playing field as the Cruiser. The night before we left, he decided that we should take two cars to the festival to accommodate all his friends' camping gear. Apparently, there were suddenly five people he needed to please. I was incredulous. I had gone to great lengths to secure our ride, had worked it all out, for god's sake: me and him in the gorgeous FJ, just the two of us jumping into this bad-ass tank, leaving town at dawn, full tank of fuel, driving into the early-morning light on a love and rock-'n'-roll adventure. I found it incredibly strange that, knowing the trouble I had gone to in order to secure our ride, he had never mentioned any of these other plans until the very last minute. Now suddenly it felt like the entire trip was about to be messed up. Dammit!

I felt like a caveman who had brought home the kill and, while I had been out hunting, everyone had ordered takeaways from the cave next door. I grew petulant and sent him a text, stating that he should go without me. That, in turn, set off a stream of virtual to-and-fro dialogue that quickly became repetitive, until I was so confused by who was saying what that I abandoned the keypad and decided to call him.

As soon as he picked up, I could tell from the background noise that he was in a bar and was well on his way to becoming completely plastered. Men who have problems with alcohol … we just couldn't seem to escape each other. But this wasn't the time to start trying to understand why every man I seemed to get involved with was a drunk. Besides, there was no need to get too hung up on gender since my mother, the Matriarch of Martinis, loomed large overhead. "Stop being so fucking judgemental," I told myself.

Clinic Boy tried to explain why we needed to take both cars. It all began to feel absurd. Finally, I convinced him that the Cruiser could accommodate a lot of equipment, that I would scale my own stuff right down and that I would pick him up at 8:30 sharp the following morning.

After I ended the call, I went off to repack, chucking out three pairs of shoes, extra towels, my woolly blanket, two camping chairs, and a Bluetooth hi-fi.

The next morning, the peak-hour traffic across Joburg was carnage, with most traffic lights down, so I was over an hour and a half late by the time I finally arrived to pick up Clinic Boy at his parents' cottage, on a palatial property with rolling gardens and a sparkling chlorine-injected pool. Nowhere better is the discrepancy between the rich and poor demonstrated but here in the Republic of the North. I catch a glimpse of "the maid", all kitted out in matching apron, hat and frock, scuttling towards the main house, carrying in the laundry from the washing line.

Clinic Boy looked a mess – a combination of sleepy, anxious and very stoned. His red vein-tracked eyes told a thousand tales of inner disturbance. The smell of dope was acrid. For a while now I had been refusing to acknowledge the signs that he was a stoner, a total stoner. I had spent many years of my life in the haze of marijuana – I knew it well. In fact, of all the drugs I have ever taken, heroin and crack included, I have come to believe that dagga is the most insidious. On my "Drugs To Give Up" list, it was definitely one of the hardest to kick.

As much as I tried to ignore it, it had become increasingly clear that when he was stoned, which was pretty much most of the time, he became vague, removed and distant. Just as Ex-Boyfriend and my mother were unable to connect to me emotionally because of the alcohol, so too with Clinic Boy and the dope. But, being a master denialist, I ignored the signs because I didn't want to see them. I was too lonely, the big black hole too big to acknowledge anything that was going to threaten to snatch away the syringe of serotonin that I was trying to fix myself up on. I couldn't stand more pain right then, not after the devastating way my barely beating little black heart had been pummelled into roadkill. I needed a love fix and I needed it now.

But the truth is hard to kill. Waves of realisations that he was perhaps not the guy I imagined him to be were beginning to crash into my brain at the least expected times. The things that I first loved about him – his gentleness, his calm serenity, his fascinating broodiness, like Heathcliff on the stormy moors – were fast becoming problematic.

Damn. That bloody Dr Imago had said it would be this way, when he warned us that after the initial honeymoon phase, when everything was soft focus and smelled of sweet roses, that we would get to a place where everything we liked about each other would turn out to be opposite. I could sense it happening but, like a madman clinging to a boat on a stormy sea, I refused to let the realisation sink in.

I needed to rescue my love, tug him back into the harbour of my heart, into the soft-focus misty ocean of my dream.

Yet reality kept kicking back, like a mad Palomino horse. And with each exposé of truth I felt my anger rising. Jesus, fuck, I had collected enough rage in the last year to power the planet with toxic light. And I could sense that his Imago reality check on me was just as brutal. What he once saw as my strength – creativity and energy – he now began to experience as control issues and mania. More than once he had told me that I criticised "everything" he did. So, while he began to dissolve into versions of my mom, distant, cut off and uncaring, I began to resemble his judging, unforgiving and controlling mother.

As he meandered around in a haze, searching for bits and pieces of camping equipment, I bit my tongue from saying, "Isn't it a bit early to be stoned right out of your mind?"

We still needed to stop at a friend's place to pick up all the other people's goods. I had a growing sense that this trip was going to have a profound effect on our relationship, that it was going to swing one way or the other – that it was going to be make-or-break kind of stuff.

The odds had slowly been stacking up: the age difference, the cultural divide – even though he was a new-breed Afrikaner, relatively liberated and open-minded compared to his racist Dutch forefathers, I felt sometimes that we remained eons apart. But I was still too lonely in my soul to make any kind of sensible call, such as, "Let's call it quits." This was the core of my disease, my codependency, showing itself in its full glory: the part of me that stayed for years and years in relationships that sapped me of energy because I was too goddamn scared of being alone. It felt like I had been doing this all my life – hanging on to the comfortably shitty numbness of familiarity, a familiarity that did nothing but breed paralysis and contempt.

But then something terrifying happened ...

Watching Clinic Boy move through his slow, disjointed dope-infused haze, I was suddenly overwhelmed by the need to join him and get high. It seemed to come from nowhere, but of course – looking back at it later – naturally, it came from somewhere. From a place that had already been set in motion a long time ago. One moment I was watching him, a sneer of disapproval lurking on my upper lip, the next I wanted to leap into and share his spaced-outness. The desire grew stronger, all but choking me. I stared at him – hungry eyed, cannibal crazy. I breathed in deep, swung my hips and sidled up to him, my breath in his ear. "I need a little sniff of what you're smoking. Please, babe, just blow some back at me, just a little whiff. I just want to smell the feel."

He was surprised, shocked even. Everyone who knows me knows that I don't do shit. No alcohol, no cigarettes, no dope, no smack, no crack, no jack. Although I'm not always serene, I am the epitome of clean.

I swung my hips a little more, pressed into him harder, wiggled and squiggled myself a little closer.

"It's not like I am going to actually smoke it," I whispered. "I won't actually touch it."

Unable to resist me, he took a deep pull and delivered a lungful of sweet, heady dope into my face. I breathed the air in. It went *downnnnn* deep, right into that black hole, the dark never-ending cave of my soul, that space that never can be fixed, that never can be filled.

One small, microsecond inhale of second-hand smoke, and oh how for a moment my demon danced. Oh, how it flew free. I shot up through that roof of normal and for a moment I flew. Flew! It felt like that first-time high, when I was 16, and the world was everything I wanted it to be.

We jumped into the Cruiser – it was joy-ride time. An hour later I told him we needed to stop. I had decided to buy a five-pack of cherry-tipped cigars. It was almost immediate, the opening of Pandora's poison box. By the time we reached Oppikoppi I had finished my first cigar. It was the first time I had smoked in over a decade.

Oh fuck. Suddenly, a lungful of terror. What the fuck am I doing here? The hole inside me had just imploded – a million miles deep and a million miles wide.

CHAPTER 15

Held Hostage by My Sobriety

The campsite is inhabited by about 12 people, most of whom are from different parts of Eastern Europe. These people really like to party, with an array of some or other mood- and mind-altering substance on tap. Dope is everywhere – it may as well be growing on bushes there is so much of it. Cooler boxes brimming with icy beers, ciders; six different types of whiskey and tequila are mainstays. In a far-off corner, lines of coke are surreptitiously snorted by the edgy diehards. By the looks of their agitation, it's highly likely that the powder is mostly cut with speed or strychnine. One of the Bulgarians has brought along a plastic container of dark chocolate mixed with magic mushrooms.

The partying goes on from morning to early morning in one long four-day, get-loaded marathon. It's kind of like *Lost in Trashlation.*

And me? I am in my own personal purgatory. Sucking on cigars, hating myself for succumbing after 10 whole fucking years of not smoking, feeling wholly unsatisfied by every long deep pull I take while all the time wanting to go leaping into the cooler box to down the whiskey, smoke five joints and snort a kilo of white. I keep telling myself, whatever you do, *do not have a cigarette!*

But, just as cancer multiplies once you cut into it, my hunger to use has grown enormous. Instead I hide away in tortured twistings and punch hateful paragraphs on my iPad, which is quickly losing battery power. I'm sure that out of the 30 000 plus revellers I must be the *only* one who is not using – unless sucking on stupid cigars counts, of course.

Clinic Boy has brought along a one-man tent and we have two sleeping bags – and little else. So much for him being the typical boer, the outdoor boy. I roll up clothes to make some sort of a cushion to ease the edge of a sharp rock under my neck. I have nothing to soften the assault on my spine that takes a bruised beating.

At about 3 am on Night One, I wake up projectile vomiting. I fail to make it outside and, instead, get trapped at the flap of the tent and so spattered puke lines the inside zipper. Mortified, I stumble out into the black night in search of my bag with wet wipes, but just as I manage to grab a handful, it all shoots out again. Now the heaving won't stop. By the time I have emptied my insides, I am left with only a sad trickle of yellow bile. Clinic Boy attempts to comfort me but he is far too blotto on whatever he has been imbibing over the past 24 hours and soon slips back into unconsciousness. I manage to wet wipe most of the evidence from the tent. I cannot help but think it is my internal defence system reacting against everything around me, all the substances and using around me, the sniffing in of the weed, the tugging at cigars. My Sobriety God is not impressed and the puking is an indication of just how "not amused" he is. I feel goddamn awful, but weirdly purged.

At Oppikoppi I soon see the Imago theory playing out in full force as Clinic Boy transforms from his former self – or at least the person I imagined him to be. Gone is the sweet, shy and gentle boy whose eyes looked like a million oceans could melt in them. Instead, I meet the closed-off, stubborn one, consumed in his smoking and beer drinking, his mission to get high. I watch myself lose touch with him as he gets lost in bong smoking and beer cracking. Increasingly, I begin to feel that I am the loneliest girl in the world.

Watching inebriated revellers at a rock festival disintegrate into blurry, blubbery versions of themselves is like watching a mob of zombie walkers tear at each other, limb for limb, until all that is left is a heap of rip-torn flesh and shuddering bones. By 2 am the walking dead are begging for redemption but mainly they just want directions to their tents and stumble around in circles, lost in some drunken haze of alcohol-induced amnesia.

Despite muttering – clearly, to myself – that I don't drink and don't smoke, I am constantly offered a beer or a joint gets passed my way. When people are drunk or high, or both, the last thing they want to deal with is some sober chick staring into nothing. I repeatedly try to make my non-using a non-issue but it is clear that here, in the middle of dusty nowhere, I am nothing but a tedious prisoner, held hostage by my own sobriety.

Despite being shoulder to shoulder with people, crashing in a camp with 12 others, one of 30 000 in one space, I have never felt so alone in my life. Like some sad, mad spinster of solitude, I belong nowhere. Thankfully, however, I have organised media accreditation, which means I can go intermittently to the tented, powered-up area to charge my iPad and phone and feign interest in interviewing inebriated wannabe rock-star musos.

Once again my writing rescues me; it's all I have to hang on to. Each time I feel the screech of social weirdness, I bury myself in my iPad and write and write and write … I have never been as aware of how writing can save a life. At Oppikoppi, my writing is like my sponsor, my therapist, my NA meeting and my Higher Power all rolled into one.

After three days of back-to-back noise, distorted music and goofballs getting progressively more wasted, we decide to leave a day early. There have been many times that I have kicked myself for resisting the plan to take two cars – I would probably have packed it all in and left after the first night if Clinic Boy had had his own ride back. As we load up the dusty gear into the back of the Cruiser and head out past the tented camp, back to the city, our forced chitchat soon sinks into silence and the distance grows and grows.

It is clear that something has changed between us. It is almost imperceptible, but it is there – like that gnawing stone in my spine that left bruise marks on my back for weeks after I returned from Oppikoppi.

I just can't seem to get the images out of my head of him getting loaded, seeped in booze and weed and whatever else was at hand. Our age gap seems insurmountable. I suddenly feel very, very old. I swear off the cigars. But the craving is intense.

CHAPTER 16

The Problem with Dating Ben 13

"Dating a younger man is tricky," my friend Monica said to me in a Skype convo from Oz. "There comes a time, just when you have grown to trust them, that you finally decide to lean on them, but they just can't take the weight."

Right from the start I had always known that Clinic Boy and I would never be a happily-ever-after story, that it was a relationship that had "end" written all over it, and that despite me saying that I didn't attach much to age, after Oppikoppi it was clear that I was too old (and too sober) for him.

"He's not my Ben 10, he's my Ben 13," I would laugh when I told people about my new boyfriend. I knew that I could never be that girl who would live in the picture-postcard house with a picket fence with him and give him babies, even though he constantly told me how healthy I was every time I bled and that he wanted me to have his child. I laughed him off, of course, knowing how ridiculous the idea was. "Grow your own baby in a test tube" was my stock response. Besides, he seemed to be walking around in circles, without direction, whirring in confusion most of the time. He barely knew what he was doing from day to day, so when he talked about procreation, it was so absurd to me that it always left me keeling over laughing.

But the real problem – his emotional unreliability – came out in full force soon after we returned from Oppikoppi. For no apparent reason, Clinic Boy went Missing in Action. Suddenly the WhatsApps stopped. The grey ticks stayed single, and when I tried to call him, his phone had been switched off.

One day turned to two, three, four days of concrete silence. No blue double-ticks.

I found myself becoming increasingly worried about him, even obsessively so. My main concern, of course, was that – given his history of depression – he had killed himself: taken an overdose, or perhaps, in a dark moment, had rigged up a rope and hanged himself.

He had been swinging more and more into the depths of depression lately, I reasoned; he'd been really erratic about taking his meds, plus he smoked far too much dope for someone with depression. And he would go off on soliloquies of self-pity, telling me of his failures as a man, as a human being, and how he was nothing more than a deep, black hole. The rants would often plummet into how he wished he could put an end to it all.

And when I was not convincing myself that he had killed himself, I was certain he had met someone else and was betraying me. Or perhaps he had just switched off, turned his back on the world, and was kicking back on a back-to-back festival of dog or some other fetish porn. What I was really sensing was his absolute emotional unreliability.

My worrying about things over which I had absolutely no control was like shooting elastic bands across virtual space in the hope of finding him but all they did was shoot right back and sting me. It felt about as worthless as watching reruns of *Keeping Up with the Kardashians*.

With Clinic Boy's sudden withdrawal, coming out of what seemed like nowhere, like a chop in the head, a knife sawing through the jugular, blood spurting like some Daniel Pearl gritty CNN news clip, I was left teetering. Our relationship appeared to be over. How could The End have happened so quickly, back-to-back with Ex-Boyfriend? Me being so defenceless, so caught off guard ...

Fuck, fuck, fucking Fuck. Why hadn't I seen it coming through those fucking little rose-tinted specs that seem to stick to my eyes like a second skin?

The result was that I went to see my therapist, Tine, at Hotel Hospital. The second I sat down on the couch, it all came out – the abandonment, the crazy OCD, the loss, the fear, his withdrawal, the drinking, his weirdness, his aloofness. I cried from 9:05 to 10 am. At the end of the session, Tine gave me an extra 10 minutes and made it clear that the side of Clinic Boy I was now encountering was the real deal: The Avoidant – withdrawn, angry and irrational. The one who could offer me nothing. This, she reminded me, was his true shadow side, that these were the parts that I would be exposed to more and more as time went by.

Matter of factly, she explained how his complexes were so deep and complicated, his inexplicable guilt and self-denial so confusing, that they were about to choke me. She thought he ticked all the boxes for someone who should be clinically diagnosed with Avoidant Personality Disorder whereby anxiety basically underpins his personality, causing social withdrawal, distance, distrustfulness and aloofness.

"Someone with APD is unable to maintain intimate relationships despite longing for closeness and connection," she told me. "They're terrified of criticism, rejection, shame and disapproval. Their behaviour, movement and speech often seem overly controlled and they view themselves as socially inept and unappealing. They constantly test people to see who can be trusted, but their actions often create mistrust because they're emotionally unreliable."

Her description read like a tailor-made character reference for Clinic Boy.

But that was not all. Just as she had diagnosed Ex-Boyfriend, she was certain that Clinic Boy was also a narcissist, just one who was more manipulative and harder to spot.

Before I left, Tine got straight to the point, and there was no doubt about what she was advising me to do: get the fuck out of there! If I stayed, smothered by all his complexes and restrictions, everything free about me, my spontaneity, my love for life, my passion, my sexuality would all be snuffed out. But perhaps the thing that that session made most painfully clear to me was my own avoidance. Finally I saw that ever since I had left the clinic, all I had been doing was hiding from my own pain, avoiding all my own built-up hurt, by spending all my energy and time on trying to understand and fix up Clinic Boy. Just as I had always done – with Ex-Boyfriend, Boy 2 and the one before and the one before him, right back to trying to fix my mother.

Fuck. Fuck. Fuck. You fucking fixer.

Finally, I had been forced to face my truth: I was terrified of confronting my self, my own pain. I lived to avoid the hole in my soul.

I drove away. Fuck. I was dying for a cigar.

CHAPTER 17

Oscar and Cigars

Straight after the therapy session with Tine, I headed directly to the convenience store that sold loose cherry-tipped cigars and bought one – just one, neatly wrapped in cellophane.

"It's okay," I told myself. "Just one and then I'll stop. At least it's not a cigarette. If it were a cigarette then I'd really be smoking," I tried to convince myself. "But this ... this is expensive and impractical. I'm hardly going to get addicted to this shit."

Denial is a motherfucker. I have come to believe that the bigger the problem, the greater the denial, the more one furiously says, "It's only a line, a drag, a sip ..." the more one is probably hiding from the truth. People who don't have a problem with addiction, don't minimise. They don't. Straight fact.

Despite having sworn off the cigars after I'd returned from Oppikoppi in August, after having consumed two boxes in three days, and managing to stay away from them in the weeks that followed, it felt as if the hungry, using beast had been unleashed in me and, in hindsight, my smoking habit started after I had lit the first one. Sadly, there was no "good behaviour" credit or parole for the 10 years I had abstained.

And just as the cigars sidled in, after he re-emerged from his Missing In Action stint – without any real explanation – Clinic Boy and I slid slowly back into our "relationship". I hardly mentioned how much he had upset and worried me when he had been on his Withdrawal Sabbatical.

With denial comes amnesia, forgetfulness. It was almost as if nothing had happened. Our WhatsApp timelines were soon full of little emoticons once again: sweet goodnights ☺ ☺ and happy good mornings ☺ ☺.

And in the middle of all of this, this smoky muddle of avoidance, came the news I had been waiting for months to hear: that, finally, a date had been set for the verdict in the case of Oscar Pistorius, the Olympic athlete accused of murdering girlfriend Reeva Steenkamp. And this meant that we could finally release the book I had been writing in collaboration with Trish Taylor, *Oscar: An Accident Waiting to Happen*. After months and months of sifting through evidence and breaks and closing arguments, Judge Thokozile Masipa would adjourn the court for four weeks and then announce the judgment that the entire world had been waiting for. The date for the court to reconvene was set for 11 September 2014.

From the moment I met up with Patricia Taylor, back at the Franschhoek Literary Festival in 2013, three months after Reeva's shocking killing, it seemed like the story of the stump-legged athlete had held me hostage. It was at the festival that Trish asked me to write a book about the year and half her family got to know the murder accused when he began dating her then 17-year-old daughter, Sam Taylor.

Over the following 10 months, Trish and I would meet in secret, in Joburg and CT, grabbing stolen moments away from work at The Magazine, recording hours and hours of interviews. I soon got to hear how initially Pistorius was respectable and charming, wooing Sam, their beautiful barely-out-of-school daughter. But over time things changed, and soon he was wreaking havoc in their lives, consumed with anger issues, lies, deception and recklessness.

I spent many months trying to order and make sense of the reams of material, shaping it into some form of coherence, in the hope of capturing the essence of a man who had captured the whole world's attention with a tragic tale of darkness, contradiction and intrigue.

And then there were the challenges of dealing with Trish, who understandably grew increasingly anxious as the trial drew to an end. She lived in constant fear that the contents of the book would be leaked and that she would end up breaking the stringent rules surrounding her responsibilities as a state witness in the trial. Added to those stresses, she was also worried that anyone of Pistorius's numerous cronies may try to harm her family – or us for writing the book. The Taylors had been threatened before Reeva's death and, with so many volatile characters in the story, anything could happen.

After The Crash, there were also growing legal concerns that the Pistorius team may try to prevent the book from hitting the shelves.

As it turned out, the book arrived from the printers at the end of March, the week before I admitted myself to Hotel Hospital. In fact, it was quite surreal for me to watch hours and hours of the trial on a couch in the clinic's lounge, alongside people who had no idea that I had written a book that was tucked away in my suitcase upstairs and was about to cause a storm.

It was, in many ways, one of the core reasons I had checked myself in: to ready myself for the media madness I knew would erupt when the Oscar verdict was announced, when our book could finally be released. Not being able to control the endless stream of tears that made me feel so emotionally unstable, before entering the clinic's doors back in early April, I knew how imperative it was that I found a way to get a grip and control myself so that when the day dawned that I needed to pitch up to appear on TV news shows and do radio and print interviews, I would be able to keep it together.

Now, with a date for the verdict announced for the week of 11 September, I essentially had 30 days before the big onslaught. So it was that I decided, in the midst of this impending overload, that I would allow myself to smoke cigars for the four weeks leading up to the verdict and the week following, and then I would stop.

It seemed simple and reasonable enough. I would afford myself five weeks of a smoking crutch and then go back to the way it was before I had relapsed on tobacco. I convinced myself that I needed something, something to suck on, something that would help me de-stress and still the beating of my brain and heart.

Drinking wasn't an option, drugging was a total no-go. I couldn't take heroin, crack, coke, tik, quat, dope, pills – but I could, I decided, light up a civilised white-tipped cherry-flavoured cigar. Plus, I would look all tough and cool like Marlon Brando or Dorothy Parker.

It's amazing how the mind works just before a relapse. It tells you: *You deserve this. You've been so good. You deserve something. At least you're not really smoking. Cigars aren't cigarettes. You'll only smoke one … maybe two at the most. You're tough, you've given up heroin. You've stayed away from nicotine for 10 years – you'll put it down in an instant, but right now you REALLY need to smoke a teeny-weeny harmless cigar to make yourself feel better.*

It was the day of the Oscar verdict and from 6 am my phone began to ring off the hook. Trish was in London with Sam doing a string of media interviews when the storm broke, so it was left to me to meet the media onslaught that imploded like a shower of rotten eggs. As the gooey mess all came down, I felt a little abandoned, and tried to cope by sucking on cigars.

It was mayhem. ABC, BBC, Chinese TV, Reuters – they were all looking for the Taylors and, since they weren't around, they were left with me. SABC, eTV, SAfm, 702, radio station after radio station were calling me. I couldn't say no – I was both author and publisher and I knew that this kind of coverage was gold. It was the zenith of Oscar mania: the world was watching, the book's sales were peaking on Amazon – we are the No. 1 new release – and I simply had to hold the fort. And, besides, I had always been a media ho, and this time round I knew how limited the window of opportunity was in terms of the high world interest, interest that would last only while Pistorius was headline news.

Plus, I had worked damn fucking hard to be first out of the stable with the Oscar book. *Oscar: An Accident Waiting to Happen* had been raring to go for months, like a rampant dark horse waiting to thunder out the stalls. In order to release it on the day of the verdict, to be unpacked and placed on the shelves in stores, I had had to plan it like some Desert Storm operation in Iraq.

It had been waiting for months like a caterpillar fit to burst, an overdue baby. With its delivery date hanging on the verdict of the case, I had taken enormous measures to comply with legal restrictions. We could not reveal a cover. We could not do a press release. We could not in any way mention Trish's name when we whispered to the head of sales at Exclusive Books that we had an "inside story" on the Oscar story. Because Trish was on the list of 103 state witnesses, the book's release before the verdict could severely damage the state's case. Sometimes late at night, when my mind was spinning chaotically, I wondered what would happen if I leaked it and was then blamed for the collapse of the state prosecutor Gerry Nel's case. The Crash would look like butterfly shit compared to this. It was something that the crazy side of me was vaguely tempted to do: cause complete chaos and let the Blade Runner book out the bag.

The truth, though, is that the entire story had left me feeling sick. I had become part of a cauldron of darkness and negativity. But at this stage there was no stopping the bus. What was done was done, and I needed to handle it all as best as possible.

As the culpable homicide verdict was delivered and much of the world was left horrified at Oscar Pistorius's lenient five-year sentence, I tried to keep a grip on things and got my hair done. I convinced myself that a GHD look would somehow keep my usual shoot-it-straight foot-in-mouth disease under wraps. I needed to be both careful and concise in media interviews. I couldn't blurt out opinions such as, "Oscar's a murderer – let the son-of-a-bitch burn in hell!"

As a result, by the time the verdict was handed out, I was smoking up a storm. The first became another became a box. People who saw me smoking after my 10-year hiatus screamed in shock. The smokers were the loudest: "What the hell d'you think you're doing? Stop!" they coughed and spluttered.

In the cloud of their nicotine haze, they were entirely oblivious to their own hypocrisy.

"That's it – you're fucked!" they hacked. "You'll never stop now. You've fallen, you've failed, you're a smoker again!" There was glee behind their sanctimonious anger.

"I haven't smoked for 10 years, fuck you!" I shouted back. "I'm only doing this to de-stress. At least I have an excuse! None of you know what fucking hell I'm going through!" I protested. "Try living in my brain for a week. It's all Oscar's fault!" I yelled.

Then my 17-year-old son caught me. After puffing like some secretive crackhead, behind the yesterday, today and tomorrow bush at the side of the house, I walked back through the front door, having forgotten to take a swig of Listermint I'd hidden in a tiny hole in the chopped-off tree trunk.

My olive-eyed son was furious.

"You smoking again?" he snarled.

"I had one ... only one," I stammered. The lie did a backflip and shimmied across the newly polished Oregon floors. "I'm stressed, I can't cope. Stop looking at me like that."

"Fuck you ... fuck you ... fuck you," he shouted. "That's it – I'm never talking to you again." He slammed his teenage bedroom door. The walls shook from floor to ceiling.

"Don't talk to me like that," I whimpered. "Don't fucking swear."

"I'm never-ever-ever coming to your house again either," my youngest son joined his brother in exiling me.

I wept. Now everybody hated me. And now I was dying to go back and puff those tears away.

"I'll stop. I promise I'll stop," I shouted into slammed doors. "I'm sorry ... I'm sorry, sorry, sorry, sorry, sorry. Please forgive me. Please understand. It's just that I'm stressed."

"That's bullshit!" My eldest emerged from his room. "You've been stressed before and you've never fucking smoked!"

He was right.

Of course he was right. So why was I doing this?

"I am stopping, I promise. I'm sorry, darlings. I promise."

And within 20 minutes of our shout-down, I was back outside, lighting up another cigarette to consider the meaning and reasons for it all. This time I didn't forget the Listermint. I also rubbed lavender leaves on my palms and fingers and sprayed Doom in my room.

All that I know is that I have never seen more clearly how addiction is a progressive disease. One becomes two becomes four becomes eight and soon the boxes are piling up. I watched helplessly as it got worse. And the denial kept setting the rules. "They're only cigars … Just don't light a cigarette. If you buy cigarettes then you're really fucked."

In an attempt to still the terrible tide, I decided to mark down a Cigar Sobriety Day – four weeks from then. Five weeks of smoking had already come and gone. Oh, how the goal posts kept shifting … Then I gave myself permission to go on a nicotine binge: a gluttonous bender of cigars. I smoked like a demon, billowing clouds thundered out of me like a scaly dragon. I smoked and smoked and smoked, smoked and smoked and smoked. I spent ridiculous amounts of money on these elegant cellophane-wrapped cherry-tipped cigars. They range in price between R24 and R30. At the airport they cost R55 a stick. The days of one or two a day quickly become a box, which cost R128 at the local supermarket.

But sometimes the box was finished by 6 pm and then I needed another. I worked out that I was now spending between R130 and R250 a day on cigars. That's about R1200 a week – over R5 000 a month on smoke! Huh? If I carried on like this I'd be spending R60 000 on cigars a year! I could have educated three children. But did these atrocious calculations stop me? Not at all. The harsh reality, when I was brave enough to look at it, just heaped more shame on me. They say that when the pain becomes too intense, we change. Clearly I hadn't been burnt badly enough yet.

The worse I felt, the more guilt I felt, the more I relished each drag, each suck, each pull. I couldn't get enough. I needed more-more-more. And I went out at all hours of the night to get my fix.

In this highly charged black-hole-of-the-soul state, each day I saw more and more parallels to the way I used to be when I was a fucked-up crack- and smackhead. It was just that my addiction was slightly more elegant now.

"You might as well be smoking heroin," my eldest son spat at me one day. "You're a drug addict. Face it. Don't tell people you're clean, cos you aren't," he snarled. "You're an addict – an addict, an addict!"

I lit up another. Right in his face. This time I didn't even bother with the lavender or Listermint.

CHAPTER 18

The Contemplation of Kicking Butt

I chose a Sunday to stop smoking.

A Sunday meant that there was no work and plenty of time to bury myself in my smoke bible, a book that once helped me miraculously stop 10 years back: *Allen Carr's Easy Way to Stop Smoking*. It had been the catalyst for my nicotine sobriety over a whole decade ago, during which time I got to joyously live life, free, as a non-smoker.

From the moment I gave up, I had no cravings and no longings. In fact, I had experienced the wonderful gift of cigarette emancipation the very second I stubbed my last one out.

So that Sunday I dropped my son off at Master Maths in Rosebank and headed for the smokers' section in the Mugg & Bean in Killarney, where I had stopped the first time. I was hopeful it would bring me luck.

The area where the coughers congregate was muggy and greenish-tinged from years of stale smoke and nicotine build-up. I had two cigars, like two rifles cocked, a soldier going to war. Instead of my dog-eared, coffee-stained copy of my smoke bible, I now had the pristine clean screen downloaded e-book ready to read on my iPad's Kindle app.

I found a table among the purple-faced blue-veined hackers. The acrid reek of smoke cut into my nostrils. I unwrapped the first cigar, ordered coffee and began to read as I lit up. I had seen these words before. A decade before they had been brand new and had elicited an incredible awakening. Now I had to work hard to find the same excitement.

I speed read. By page 60, I was done. I didn't need to read to the end. I had got it. I was done. I crushed the last third of the smelly cigar. Yes, I was done. I took a photo of the cigar, crushed in the ashtray, and posted it on Instagram. I announced to my followers: *Day 1 clean #nicotine free*.

That was pretty easy. I felt the glow. I was a pro at giving up things. I paid the bill and walked out, cigar free and elated. How easy was that? Easypeasy, I smiled smugly.

I told my boys that their mama had returned to the fold of the smokeless. I could see they were slightly dubious but they were also thrilled. I texted Clinic Boy: *I am free*. My momentary lapse into the dungeon of smoke was over. Now I was done. Tra-la-la-laaa.

When I got to work on Monday I watched the smokers scuttle out for their hourly smoke in the designated downstairs smokers' area outside. I felt sorry for them. Poor slaves to the cancer stick. But, just to make sure that I really did get it, I opened the book again. By 11 am I was feeling grouchy, lethargic and edgy. What the fuck? This hadn't happened last time. Withdrawal, clearly. *What the fuck?* I couldn't sit still. The craving ants were biting me, gnawing at my skin. I watched the nicotine prisoners leave to get their fix again, and this time I was horrified by how much I envied them. My heart was racing, mind longing to join. It was not fucking working. I was not supposed to be feeling this! Maybe it was because I had jumped the gun and hadn't read to the end. I picked up the iPad, and I tried to concentrate, to focus on page 61.

"If you haven't stopped smoking at this point, keep smoking till the end."

I read the sentence over and over again.

It was telling me to smoke. Huh? I didn't see that last time – it was telling me to smoke. The words were twisting all my resolve to stop. It was amazing how my mind was just sucking in this new information.

A delicious rush of anticipation spilled over me. I got up, automated, like a machine that has no will of its own. Picked up the keys to my test Audi 3 cab and headed for the parking lot. Like a zombie, I pulled into the nearby Engen garage, and bought a single cherry-tipped cigar: R27.50.

My palms were sweaty as I unwrapped it and lit up. I inhaled the heavenly cherry ... I was home.

Oh fuck. Head rush. As I drove back to the office my head whirred.

The self-loathing quickly followed – and proceeded to swallow me up.

"What a loser, what a weakling! Look at you – you can't fucking stop. Not even 24 hours. *Relapse Baby!* You're hooked. Tarred, lined and sunken ..."

In a few days I was to celebrate 15 years in sobriety. And, for the first time in my recovery, I was dreading it.

* * *

I puffed and puffed and puffed on that cherry-tipped cigar in the car before I entered the NA meeting in Norwood where I was to do my 15-year clean-and-sober share. I thought about this decade-and-a-half birthday. Because, far more than marking clean time, it was the first-year anniversary of The Crash, the cacophonous soundtrack to my life that was going to accompany me in some or other way to the very end of it. It still felt like yesterday: the rush of flashbacks, heart surges and images that streak like lightning on the blackboard of my mind. There had been no solace, nothing anyone had been able to say or do to make me feel better. It was there at the back of my mind all the time, before sleep, in dreams and in waking. It had never really left my side, the terror, that near-death sense of it all and then the twisted guilt and fear. Was this what I had become? The full sum of my fears?

I glanced at myself in the rear-view mirror, stared at the reflection in the glass. The more broken I felt inside, the more perfect I tried to look on the outside. The new sleek-as-silk hairstyle, my iPad Air, my new Samsung phone, all the perfumes lined up in a row: Issey Miyake, Chanel, Tom Ford. The floor-to-ceiling closets pregnant with too many clothes, too many wedges, stilettos, flats, trainers, boots, pumps; too many books, anti-wrinkle creams, Facebook friends, Twitter followers, Instagrammers. It felt like my life had become a giant hoarding safe-deposit box, collapsing under the weight of everything I had toiled and sweated for. Like a frozen Botox bitch, the outsides were taut with perfection, while inside the poison built up and pushed against my cell walls. Trying to find an outlet. And while my friends and followers on social media kept cooing and congratulating me, the sense that I was little more than a downtown China mall fake just kept growing stronger and stronger.

What would I share at my fifteenth birthday? My life felt like a litany of disasters. Surely I should be better than what I am? A car accident? A three-week stay in a clinic? A fucking nervous breakdown? A slow puncture? An implosion? A new addiction to nicotine? A Bipolar diagnosis, and a prescription of meds?

I contemplated turning the ignition and reversing out of the parking lot, not pitching, doing a no-show. My pride was telling me to stay away ... It would be the first year that I would miss my birthday.

I decided to fuck the fear and do it anyway.

I took a few final puffs and felt the congealed thick-as-tar-slime shame lace the pit of my lungs as I made my way to my seat in the circle of addicts. Young and old, rich and poor, black and white: crackheads, pinkos, dopeheads, quat-heads, smackers, methies all in one place. This fucking nicotine thing was seriously messing with my head. But, looking around me, I was not out of place. Most of the recovering addicts in the room were inhaling 20 to 60 cigs into their lungs a day in the eternal quest for serenity.

I feared that my struggle with nicotine might be lost on them but decided to do what I had always done when sharing: speak from the heart, no matter how bleak or "unpopular" that may be – tell the truth, because it's in the telling of it that we are set free.

So rather than portray myself as the perfect all-knowing addict who has stayed clean for years, countless 24-hour days, who's written books on addiction and recovery and done numerous well-paid corporate motivational talks, regarded by some as somewhat of an authority on addiction, I decided to throw a zap sign to caution, reputation and pride.

And so it was that I took a deep breath and began to tell a room packed with addicts about the day after my fourteenth clean birthday, 2 September 2013 – about the high of starting the day in the gleaming red R3.2-million Italian car, which just hours later had been smashed into an unrecognisable heap of scrap metal. My story plummeted into tales of post-traumatic terror, brain-numbing insomnia, unstoppable weeping and flashbacks, legal nightmares, a humiliating break-up, misguided post-break-up sex, the catching of the Dutch lesbian in his bed. It took a brief detour into snapping dick episode, then a sharp left to the clinic, the three weeks of convalescing after a nervous breakdown ...

Once I had started it was as though I was on an autobahn of honesty – I did not stop. I just let it all out. The struggle with the Bipolar 2 diagnosis, the inner battle with the pharma meds, the panic attacks, the memory loss, I spared none of the lurid details. After almost an hour of talking, I ended by announcing to the room of dead-silent addicts that I had always believed that, as we got cleaner, we got more "Get out of jail free" cards from the stresses and traumas of life. The room hung onto every word I said. I looked each one in the eye, told them how wrong I had been – how my fifteenth year of recovery had been by far the hardest one I had ever had to endure.

I managed to croak out the tail end of my story, the bit about going to Oppikoppi and being the only clean and sober person in a crowd of 30 000 party diehards. And how I returned with a R1 000-a-week cigar habit. And how I was really struggling to kick nicotine.

Then I took a deep breath and finished off with: "My name is Melinda, I am still an addict. Thanks for letting me share."

CHAPTER 19

Good Morning, Dar es Salaam

Smoking or Non-smoking? I stared at the hotel accommodation forms I needed to fill out for the trip I was embarking on, the CNN journo awards in Dar es Salaam, Tanzania. I had now been smoking for about eight weeks and each week I told myself that I'd stop "next week". The hype of Oscar was all but over, so that was no longer an excuse, but when it comes to addiction, it's amazing how the goal posts keep shifting and how many deceits a brain can conjure up.

Usually lightning quick at making decisions, I deliberated over the smoking/non-smoking issue for days. I finally told myself that if I tick the *Non-smoking* box, that would be an incentive and I would have no choice but to have stopped by the time I got there. But I regretted my decision even before the ink had dried. Once I had scanned and mailed the form, I immediately wanted to submit another version – on which I'd ticked *Smoking*. Finally, fully aware that I was driving myself mental, I decided that if I really, *really* needed to I'd try to swop rooms when I got to the front desk of the hotel.

"You could even smoke out the window," my addiction whispered seductively to me.

Of course, when I left for Dar a week later, I had not kicked the cigars. In fact, I was now onto a R200, one-and-a-half-box-a-day habit.

I arrived a day later than the rest of the media contingent so I was alone when I landed in Dar es Salaam, the capital port city of Tanzania. It was already night-time, yet as I left the plane, the heat and humidity almost choked me. I was dying for a smoke, so after making my way through customs, I dashed outside and lit up on the pavement, instructing my cab driver to give me a few minutes so I could feed my demon.

The trip through the main roads of the city, to the sky-high revolving restaurant where a banquet was being held to welcome all foreign dignitaries and media, was only a few miles from the airport but the traffic jams in Dar are some of the worst in the world.

It took us over 90 minutes to travel fewer than 10 kilometres so halfway through the journey I bribed the driver two dollars to let me light up a cigar. I convinced myself I was a rock star in a limo en route to a concert in an exotic foreign land.

By the time I reached the function venue, half the speeches had already been made, and I tried to slip unnoticed into a room of hundreds of strangers dressed to the nines. My unease with unfamiliar situations was at an all-time high. My eyes searched for a familiar face, but it was too dark to see so I headed into the fog of people.

These situations often throw me ... No drink to clutch onto to ease the dis-ease. My cigars, my smoke crutch, wriggled seductively in my bag. Should I look for a smokers' section before I even found a table to sit at? Get a grip, I scowled at myself.

Then something drew me to a table of funky, young black women. They smiled and welcomed me.

I pulled up a chair next to Nina, who works for a foreign broadcast agency, and we started chatting – it was as though we'd known each other for years. Almost immediately I told her I needed to smoke. We finally found a tiny glass cubicle, right on the edge of the revolving restaurant, reserved for the puffers who kept nipping out for a nicotine fix. I was once again reminded how uncool it is to smoke these days. If you're lucky you find some grimy little smoke cubicle hidden away from the general population. For a second, I imagined what would happen if drinkers were treated to the same isolation.

As I unwrapped my cigar, I found myself telling Nina the whole story – of how I'd stopped for 10 years and how I'd now started again. In fact, lately I'd been telling everyone and anyone the same old blah-blah-blah every time I lit up. As if my decade of not smoking somehow excused my relapse. We spent the next hour going backwards and forwards between our table and the dingy smokers' cubicle. We shared stories about my addiction and her brother, the addict. Every family has at least one …

We spoke of our mothers and how we had lost them both to cancer, about love and unhappy relationships gone wrong. Then I told her of The Crash, showed her the two shocking photos of the aftermath I still carried with me, explained how the Ferrari had spun out of control, of my near-death experience and of how the white light swathed us and saved us. Then I moved on to my broken heart, the clinic and my breakdown.

All the time she just sat quietly and listened.

"I don't know if you believe in God, but I believe that when a person is made for important things, there's a battle between dark and light – it's mapped out from the beginning. The dark tries to capture souls who are great and throws many challenges at them. The dark tries to eat you, tries to take your soul. Addicts are usually very good people to start with, and they go through many tests. The better a soul, the greater the tests." She looked intensely at me.

"You have conquered so much, passed many tests. God is not letting go of you – you have too much light around you. Stop being so hard on yourself. Smoke – you won't do this forever. You will stop. But stop punishing yourself."

By the time I finally got to the hotel to check in, there were no smoking rooms available. So I found myself hanging out of a window on the thirteenth floor of the Hyatt Regency in Dar, puffing away from within my room for the following two days.

But for the first time in ages, I did not berate myself. For the rest of the trip, I just let it be and gave myself permission to enjoy the moment. *One smoke at a time.*

CHAPTER 20

Love Crash

Two days after I returned from Dar, I found myself at my desk at The Mag. It was a Tuesday and I was wearing my elegant navy-blue lace dress, an outfit that made me feel like a million bucks walking down the latte-bland corridors, pretending I worked for *Vanity Fair*. It was 3 pm and I was editing copy for a sex story for the December issue. It was only October but in magazines we have these crazy deadlines, working two to three months ahead. The story was called "The Ultimate Christmas Quickies", and because it was syndicated from the UK I needed to localise all references, such as change *Snog away from the snow near the fire* to *Grope outside as the summer night swelts*.

My job at The Mag had become my ATM, my way to pay the bills. But, to be honest, I had grown tired of the predictability, the emptiness of being a machine copy creator. My fingers typed letters that resembled words into inanities like: *How to turn your man on in five fast moves* or *What to do if he's cheating* or *Make him commitment ready*, *Get a bikini ready body in 5 days*, *Detox your friendships, careers, your life*. The stories had become endless babbles of clichés that I'd become robotically equipped to spew out. I guess it happens in any job when you've overstayed your time. If I wasn't an author on the side, I would probably have long since leapt off the corrugated roof of the fifth floor or at least injected myself with a vial of morphine.

Then my phone whistled: WhatsApp. Clinic Boy. He wanted to know if he could come over and see me later. I felt a twinge of worry, concern, but immediately disregarded it. I still got a little rush when I saw his name flash up on my phone. He was such a tortoise, a Missing in Action emotional avoidant, that when he reached out like that it felt like an event. Even at times a blessing.

We had spent the previous night together. It had been a little strained and, as we lay in bed smoking, I wanted to ask him why there was a sudden cavern of distance between us and whether something had happened while I had been away. I did eventually say, "It's weird – I can usually get into your head, but tonight I can't … there seems to be a block."

Of course, what I had really wanted to ask was, "Are you hiding something from me? Why are you so different, so distant tonight?" But I had stopped myself. It was probably nothing. How many times in my life had I stopped the question. Blocked the instinct. Only to find out that my intuition is always right.

I had tried to touch him. He'd pushed my hand away. "What's wrong?" He said he was soft.

"Softy!" I'd laughed playfully. "Don't worry – I'll change all that."

We began to kiss. Those long, languid, all-embracing kisses that suck me into an ocean and lift me to the sky. I felt movement. I began to play a game.

"I don't feel like sex tonight."

My hand slowly made its way to his hardening cock.

"Don't worry, that's not what I am here for."

I smiled. He got harder.

I was strangely drawn to this part of him, this non-available part. The shy, complex, tortured man. The one who needed so much reassurance. All fragile, like some glass-blown swan in a mahogany cabinet that must be handled with extreme care. Last night I had found it weirdly endearing in him. But there were times it had been a source of crazy frustration and even repulsion. But on the whole, I guess I was intrigued. I had never met a man who was so openly not okay about stuff that a lot of men simply hide and cover and lie about.

Lately, I'd been seeing flashes of his real potential. Gentle but firm, confident and even a little controlling. It was early October; we'd been together for five months – far longer than any of the shrinks at the clinic had predicted.

So Clinic Boy came over later, as arranged. He was stoned, eyes glazed, his dry mouth sandpapering all ability to speak. It was clear from his red-tracked eyes that he'd relocated to another country, the one they call High Land. There was a strange feeling in the room. Cemetery silent, everything felt dead cold. I waited for him to talk.

He was nervous – I almost felt sorry for him. All chained up in pain and agony.

"Okay, so what's up? Spit it out – tell it like it is." I stared at him. "You said you needed to talk. I'm waiting."

Finally, finally, he opened his Gobi Desert of a mouth. I could hardly make out what he was trying to say. I heard something that sounded vaguely like, "I've been obsessing about another woman."

It was like some choking confession. I tried hard to follow, but I was confused.

I was working hard on staying detached, but Hypomania wanted the low-down, to know the five Ws and an H. Who? What? Where? When? Why? And How? Dammit. I wanted details, motherfucker. I'm a writer. Spill it out like a blood river of confession, I wanted to scream. I wanted *Blood and Guts in High School* Kathy Acker stuff.

It seemed extremely hard for him to talk. I gave him a drink. Offered leftover lasagne. Dammit, why was I still mothering this fat cheating blob?

We moved back to the bedroom. I remember "Blame Game" by Kanye, with John Legend on the piano, was playing. It seemed too appropriate. I moved onto Brahms – some crazy *sturm und drang* drama. Violins, cellos, big kettle drums. We might as well have a cool sound track to accompany the ripping of the Temple of Love, I thought.

His silences were far too long and sombre for my liking, and his stony glaze was beginning to piss me off.

"So tell me ... how long has this been going on – this so-called obsession?" I could have searched for Marvin Gaye on the iPod but that would have broken into a sentence that I was hoping he was about to stutter.

Finally.

"I've liked her for a long time. I've always wanted to have something with her but she was in a long-term relationship so I could never do anything."

Oh dear, how very sad. Shall I bring out the Kleenex?

I couldn't help it – Bitchsheba comes out like daggers.

"She contacted me last week to fix her computer. I did, and then we got talking. Went for a walk. Then she started WhatsApping me. Confiding in me."

Ahhh, how sweet. How cosy.

"So, have you fucked her?" I spat it out. That's really all I wanted – or needed – to know.

"No, I haven't."

"Kissed her? Touched her?"

"No."

I wanted to believe him.

"But I have been having sexual thoughts about her ... obsessing about her."

Aah, okay, so this is what? A betrayal of the mind?

I yelped a sob. I felt a cocktail of anger and pain surge up inside me ... Then everything became detached. I was in full control again. It was like I was watching a movie of my life. Heartbreak Tuesday.

But that strength, that determination lasted only a few seconds – then I crumpled, rejected. Again. I felt a rush of blood to the head. Pins and needles in the brain. Fuck this medication. Couldn't it even allow me to feel a pure, honest psycho thought.

He began weeping, wailing about how screwed he was. He said he was afraid that if he left this house we would never see each other again.

I'd had enough. He was right. He needed to get the fuck out of my space. I suddenly felt a deep urge to write, to grab my iPad and spit it out. Capture my mind. Hold it down-down-down and drown in the detachment of words.

Jesus. Fuck. How could this be happening to me: two fucking lovers in six months! How can I be getting dumped again? What the fuck? This little dick was lucky to be with me. I was supposed to leave *him*, many times over, but instead I found myself left behind again.

I looked at him and tried to build a wall against his tears. Dammit, those saline fuckers were beginning to reach out to me, to touch me.

Then I found myself on his lap, holding him, fitting into him like a key in a padlock. The love rushing out of me into him. I couldn't help it. I wanted to love him. I wanted to kill him.

Weep, weep, weep. We wept – and then I leapt away. Detached again.

I was once again the stony, jealous witch. I couldn't get my head around it. He had chucked all this away for a *possibility*? On some whim, a "Can you fix my computer and go for a walk?" Although, actually, I wasn't sure if I believed any of that bullshit. It all seemed like a muddy puddle of rubbish.

"Is she beautiful?"

"Yes, she is."

That hurt.

I wanted to ask: is she fat? As though that could somehow make me feel better.

But I couldn't, so instead I said: "Actually, just leave. Please go. I don't want to ever see your stupid, ugly, fat face again."

It was over. The Brahms concerto ended in a triumphant bang of kettle drums. In my heart, I was howling, a mixture of rage and rejection gathering momentum, like it was killing me.

"This music is freaking me out," he said.

"Good. It's telling you to go. So please fuck off."

The reality of everything was beginning to overwhelm me, the grief getting to me.

My tears tumbled out.

"Fuck you. I gave you my most precious gift. I gave you my trust. Now you really need to fucking go."

He got up to leave. But, in truth, I wanted a minute longer. That hug again. A kiss. "Last Kiss." Eddie Vedder.

But then "This monkey's gone to heaven" came on. The Pixies.

"All I feel now is death," I mumbled to no one in particular, staring at a square of nothing. Like a mad person with electrodes probing my head. Like a gowned-up patient in Hotel Hospital. He looked at me, his eyes spilling with tears. Overwhelmed, he stood up to leave.

I opened the gate. I closed it. He was gone, like he had never been here.

I stepped over the shards of a pink glass vase, blown over by a windstorm earlier, now in pieces. Dead sunflowers lay across the stairs.

By the time I got back to the bedroom, Michael Stipe's haunting "Leaving New York" was playing, reminding me how it's often easier to leave than be left behind.

I turned the music off. Picked up my phone. Flipped to WhatsApp. Typed.

That which was broken I began to grow again, my faith and trust. It spread its little roots into the soil, your soil and my soul and little by little the shoots came, sprang green and grew into a big yellow Sunflower and now you have destroyed it. Fuck you.

Then I clicked Delete.

I logged in on Facebook. Of course I did. Where else do you go to find out how the girl you've just been dumped for looks? I searched through his paltry collection of 60 friends. The picture of the two of us in happy times – 10 days ago – was still on his wall. I wished I could delete it.

She was easy to find. There was a new girl liking all his posts. The little thumbs-ups were like fingers pointing and cooing. All vitriolic and confirming the fat squidgy lie.

He was right. She was beautiful. A small, red-haired elfin girl with tattoos everywhere. Everywhere. Back, front, sides. Nose ring, piercings. She looked gorgeous, bright, interesting. And she was talented too. She could paint. Like fucking, wow! I was blown away. Fuck. I could definitely have gone for her if I was into girls. I didn't blame him.

So, instead of being threatened, I was momentarily relieved. Hugely relieved. Instead of being demoralised, incensed by envy, I was impressed. Very. Jeez, if he could actually get this girl I'd be amazed. If he could actually nab her, I'd be the first to congratulate him. Cheers, bro! High-five, baby. But somehow, knowing what I knew about him, I very much doubted it. This fisted-up man with so many hang-ups and inconsistencies. He was such a loser.

But at least he had good taste in women. Me and her. Stupid consolation prize – like the certificate you get in Grade 4 for "Progress".

I could so easily have been her friend, vibed with this woman, the Russian Tattoo Girl. And, if by some miracle he did actually end up living happily ever after with her, at least I hadn't been replaced by a dog …

I left her home page and stared at my profile pic. I suddenly felt old. Very old.

CHAPTER 21

Back to the Start

The morning after I got dumped, I loped back to Hotel Hospital to see Tine. For a moment, there was a part of me that thought of checking back in and rejoining the slipper-and-nightgown parade, the electrode pack. To slip into my leopard-print onesie from London, eyeballs high to medicated heaven and just slide slowly away, like when the sun licks up dew on a cloudless summer day.

I had once experienced that imperceptible slip off the grid of life when I wound up on the homeless farm, back in 1999. But after the initial shock of realising where I was, that I had failed – monumentally – in the eyes of my friends, family and society, I got used to it. I'd often hum Beck's "I'm a loser baby, so why don't you kill me" on minus-degree mornings as I fetched wood to light the fire for the decrepit kitchen boiler. There had been something uplifting, hydrogen light, about no longer having to pitch up for life.

"I'm not sure how I'm going to get through all this psychic pain," I wailed to Tine. I hated the way I was feeling. Like a double dose of Narcissist Boyfriend Nightmare mixed with Avoidant Fat Boy Rejection on the rocks. I saw, once again, why I had been such a dedicated smackhead. By chasing the dragon, sucking up all the sweet Jane smoke, all my feelings could evaporate into a cloud of painless morphine chloroform.

All I had now was a big dose of Dystopian Desperation mixed

with a rough choke of cigar. All I wanted to do was run, cover, hide, duck, kill the tears and the fears. I sensed that drop-dead plummet into blackness, and I was terrified of it. Terrified to find myself back in that teary, bottomless pit of nowhere.

It felt like the blackness had been a recurring pattern all my life, ever since my father keeled over at my bony four-year-old feet; I never seemed to see the darkness coming – not until it had swallowed me whole, leaving me shocked by the deathly end of things, reeling and splattered on the rocks.

I suppose, as it is in a head-on collision, one can never really see The End. It can't be marked, signposted with a warning signal like, *Roadworks Ahead*. For something to really be an ending, it must come with an element of some surprise. Like an axe to the head.

Vulnerable, skinless, with barely a layer intact over my already battered post-Boyfriend heart, it felt as though I was plummeting into another ravine of loss as Clinic Boy and I came to an end. It cut me deep. I found myself staring into a pit of black, bottomless days. It wasn't as if I hadn't been warned by the doctors at the clinic and concerned friends. But when had I ever listened to people who knew better than me?

And then the anger began to well up, a rage that had been silent all these years like a melancholy, adolescent Tori Amos song. My emotions veered between near-psychotic fury and terrible morbidity that stretched to the depths of a bottomless lake of tears.

I was haunted by the memories of our closeness, the sweetness and the honesty we once shared and how, in an instant, it had gone up in a puff of smoke – puff-puff-puff, like the embers of my cigar when it smoulders out in an overflowing ashtray.

But more than sadness and loss, the overwhelming feeling was one of dark shame for being left high and dry and abandoned.

The shame of being alone … Why do I keep returning to it? Not the aloneness, per se, but the terrible shame I feel around it. Like some kind of red-flag target dress that sends me blindfolded to the village square to be mocked and side-lined.

In therapy, I hit a light-bulb moment on where all this shame comes from.

My mother. The one who brought me into this world, who I have carried around with me all my life, like a sad handbag. Of course. It's usually our mothers, isn't it?

Embedded in the fear ventricles of my heart are memories of my earthly maker who, suddenly widowed without warning at the age of 33, was left to fend for herself and her four young children, all under the age of 10. This had become my heritage bedtime story.

Over the years that followed my father's unexpected death, every time we met strangers, my mother would somehow find a way to introduce herself as "a widow", a woman stranded with four children to take care of. My mother's aloneness was drummed into us like a dripping tap. Day in and day out, we were reminded of her solitary confinement, like Bobby Sands locked up in a cell on some god-forsaken hunger strike, and how it was all our fault. Like an unwanted guest, that shame and guilt at causing her such pain grew like cancer, and came to stay.

Then, having been left untimely, abandoned in the shadow of my father's sudden death, the mountain of amber brandy bottles grew around us. They became her silent lover, her unconditional, non-critical companion, to salve her grief. And I took that with me, swallowed it deep inside – that shame of my mother's – and carried it into the world like an unwanted pregnancy.

I thought of Clinic Boy, about our love crash and how the week held such devastation. It amazed me how, in a few short hours, there had been such a sudden implosion of order. How could something that felt so good, so loving and pure be so badly damaged in an instant?

And then I had another epiphany of sorts, albeit a cliché I'd heard many times before. Damaged people damage people. Hurt people hurt people. I have written countless stories about the notion for The Magazine. But now, for the first time, I got it – that light-bulb moment when it penetrates, grows roots of revelation right into my brain.

Clinic Boy had no way of telling what his actions would bring, because his lifelong damage tape ruled his instincts and the decisions he made. The tape he had playing inside himself told him that what was good for him was bad. And what's bad for him was good. He could then justify doing something that would in all likelihood damage him (and others), shake his sanity, and still validate his actions as the right thing to do. He was driven by a deep need, a pull towards rejection and pain, towards that familiar place of bad. He was trapped in the loop. The more I had accepted him for who he was, the dark sides of him, the weirdness and all the craggy edges, the parts of which he was so ashamed, the more he was consumed by how wrong all that love was. The more I had made a home for him in my arms and heart, the more he wanted to tear it down. Every time I gave him love and compassion, his mind would retreat like a vampire tossed into the light. Deep in his bones, he experienced this as out of sync with what he really believed he was and what he really deserved.

I was almost freed by this revelation. His hurting me had been neither conscious nor intentional. In fact, it had nothing to do with me. He was simply unable to do anything different. Hurt people hurt people.

Perhaps adopted people, especially men, are even more affected by the deep rejection they experience in utero. By the mother who conceived them, who could not wait for the nine months to push the unwanted out and get rid of it – to hide the baby in the bottom drawer. And I have had two in a row. Ex-Boyfriend and Clinic Boy. Both, in some way, stayed faithful to their biological or adoptive mothers and, perhaps, could not help but cheat on the woman they are with.

In the same breath, however, I know enough about recovery to realise that it's easy to look at other people's problems so that you don't have to look at your own. So, for a moment, I tore my eyes away from taking their inventory and looked deep and hard within: what is this damage in me? Am I so drawn to rescuing my own mother from her pain and drinking that I make the same mistakes, the same ones, over and over again, by gravitating towards the motherless dudes again and again? This feeling of fear and abandonment ran deep.

And then, on the first Friday alone in ages, without a boyfriend, I was forced to confront my solitary confinement, my Friday-night phobia – that one night of the week when I imagine everyone is out there, laughing, dining, partying, in love and fucking. So in order to assuage the big black hole inside, to conquer the idea that the rest of the world is on Happy Hour, I decided to meet a friend for an early Thai dinner on a lonely end-of-a-week night in October.

CHAPTER 22

Tinder

Oh, Tinder. Where do I beginder?

It had been a week since Clinic Boy had dropped the sudden-death bombshell and I was sitting at a pavement table in Parktown North with Val. She's one of those priceless friends who has stayed in my life over many years despite thousands of miles of separation. An avid traveller and long-distance runner, she's one of the few people I know who can sit through a whole night of my whingeing, self-pitying, licking-my-wounds stories and still keep loving me.

Over plates of Pad Thai and Dim Sum, I told her everything, every sordid detail. Thankfully, I had cried enough tears over the previous seven days that I was now in tough, dry-eyed mode. I muttered how Clinic Boy was a tosser and how I was dying to meet someone else, to move on. Val raised her eyebrows, concerned.

I told her I was thinking of going the online dating route just to see what was out there. I asked if she knew anything about how the Tinder site works. Val knows a lot of things about a lot of stuff and explained how Tinder, linked to Facebook, loads up all your info, such as your "Likes" and friends from FB, and links you geographically to people in a set radius and within the age limits you have specified.

Despite having done almost everything deviant there is to do on the planet, from being a sleazy crack- and smackhead, to standing on street corners for my drugs, I had never done online dating. Up until then I had made a mockery of all of those sites and labelled those who frequent them a pack of pathetic, desperate losers.

But that night, with my lonely, achy feelings telling me to do whatever it took to ease the pain, I was listening closely. Once we had finished dinner, I drove home in a blur and headed straight to bed. It was only 9 pm.

Tucked up safely under my duvet, I imagined the world out there – partying, flirting and fucking. I imagined dysfunctional Clinic Boy suddenly flourishing in a bar, uncharacteristically the life and soul of the party, losing himself in slow kisses with Tattoo Girl. Like the kisses we had once shared.

So, driven by the confines of my *All by myself* Friday-night loser-girl blues, I decided to click my way to the App Store and search for Tinder. Tinder fucking Tinder. Where do I beginder?

Within a minute the app had downloaded and bang-bang-presto I was in the vortex of endless pictures of people looking for love, looking for a connection. An orange flame, an orange flame, a penny for your heart – these are the signs and symbols of our age. Our loveless rage.

I loaded my main profile pic, me in a black polo neck, looking semi-decent – not a hint of flesh or sleaze. Then I chose four other photos, all flattering in their own way, for the "gallery" and debated a description of myself.

I had 500 characters in which to write a description of me. Jeez, what does one put on a fishing line of love that's trying to hook a barracuda?

I finally came up with something that didn't sound too cheesy but intelligent and interesting, verging on the whacky to draw in like-minded folk.

I pound them out:

Not sure why I am doing this. I guess I am lost and curious. I write. I think. I talk. I read. Books. I like being alive. I ♥ tea. Apple. Samsung. Can't handle alcoholics. I like my mind unleashed. I test drive beautiful cars. Can talk NM and RPM.

I knew I was coming from a place of loss, not the best position to be in when you're looking for love, but I sensed that I was but one of the millions in the land of Tinder – heart-broken, rejected, sliced open – needing something to salve the wounds of the aorta.

I sifted through the pictures like it was a catalogue of meat. But I was very picky. Of the 40 I scanned through, I liked only four. Well, I didn't even really *like*-like them. I just liked them more than the other horrors I flicked through. By the profiles of possible Tinder suitors, it seemed like there wasn't a brain cell to share between them.

Lines such as ...

Choose your adventure.
Swipe right or you'll never know.
Unassuming but always surprising in so many ways.
Never a dull moment.
Don't complain about the dark if you are not prepared to switch on the light.
Single, easy-going. No hang-ups. Would be nice to have a nice lady by my side.

And what was with all the cyclists and sky divers? All the dudes with rifles, hugging lions, dogs, cats and cheetahs, brandishing fish and babies. Do they seriously think women will be endeared to them because they are holding cute, cuddly things? I was revolted. Then there were the steroid gym-ripped crew. Oil-drenched muscles dripping into the screen. What really killed me was the amount of men who were either with women in their pics or had cropped them out – really badly, too, so that strands of her hair still show on his shoulder. Like some unruly birthmark.

All at once, I was filled with hatred for humanity. I hated myself even more. Like Kurt in "Lithium" when he sang of being ugly, and how it's okay because all of us are. I'm looking for Nirvana in this hellhole.

I thought back to the long, dreamy conversations I'd shared with Clinic Boy in the nest of his bed, reading 13 TS Eliot poems back to back in one night – from the "The Waste Land", some from the play *Family Reunion* and the whole of "The Love Song of J Alfred Prufrock", then hardly coming up for air before diving into Ezra Pound. After reading *These fought in any case* – from the poem "Hugh Selwyn Mauberley" – and "In the Old Age of the Soul", we Googled Pound's life story. We were entranced by how he had been locked away in a sanitarium in Washington because of the subversive anti-American words he uttered and wrote during the war. Some nights, we had watched all our favourite movies, at least three of which we share in our Top 10 of all time – *Fight Club*, *Vanilla Sky*, *Eraserhead* – then switch back-to-back seasons of *The Simpsons*. We'd ODéd on music that sent us on faraway journeys to the other side of the cosmos. The deep and probing conversations into the dawn, about the disconnected world in which we found ourselves and how dark a black hole the soul can be.

How was I ever going to find a conversationist, a companion of the mind, in this tangled mess I saw before me night after night as I sifted through Tinder? I would then sniff my tears away, and keep flicking through picture after picture of all The Lonely People. *Where do they all come from?* Fuckit.

And then one night, it popped up. Ex-Boyfriend's profile.

My finger froze. Was I shocked, repelled or intrigued? It was like unexpectedly seeing a naked picture on a friend's phone. It somehow felt wrong to see him here. His photo did him little justice. He looked a bit insane, standing next to a big, pink stuffed rabbit and laughing like a loon. You couldn't even see his dreads. Where were his beautiful dreads, the dreads that had dragged me in 10 years ago and had me returning over and over again?

But his description of himself drew me in. Funny, witty, sardonic. I stared some more. My mind clicked the pieces together. So he must be out on the market again, looking for sex. Not for love. He didn't do love … I immediately concluded that his dick was probably in one piece again – they had given him six months for recovery and six months had gone by.

Images of that weekend between us flashed. The feeling of the chaos around "That Last Shag" left me nauseous. I was ashamed at how shallow I had been, how little I had cared for myself during that awful time, how I had given into him so easily in the quest for flesh, how little respect I had had for myself.

I suddenly felt sad. For both of us. Lonely idiots, rowing in circles, looking like fools for love and sex. Almost without thinking I swiped him to the right – to the "I like you" pile. Immediately after, I was "Oh my fucking fuck, why did I do that?" How shallow was I still?

The actual idea of ever being back with him after all that had happened between us, after all those years of numbing pain, made me feel really ill.

For the rest of the night, I compulsively checked out the seemingly endless pack of images on the Orange Flame Love app, to numb my brain, my pain. Maybe I was also checking to see if Ex-Boyfriend had swiped me right. Me and my stupid, stupid pride. I swiped an entire room full of men left-left-left in a frenzy of rejection. There was something excruciatingly empowering about being so brutal, swiping an entire battalion of men to the loser pile. But the more I swiped the emptier I felt.

I was swamped by sadness for the whole fucking loveless, lonely world. But of course I knew that the way I saw the world was the way I saw myself. So, most of all, I felt sad for me.

CHAPTER 23

The End of a Chapter is Not the End of the Book

SCHISM
Synonym: division, split, rift, breach, rupture,
break, separation, severance, estrangement,
alienation, detachment

They say the truth sets you free, but sometimes it hurts a fuck load
before you taste the sweet juice of liberation. How many times
does one have to travel the same terrain, experience the same pain,
before you come to the conclusion that it's "Game over – 6-love.
I'm done"?

What I found hardest to digest about the end with Clinic Boy
was how wrong I had been about him, how quickly the kind,
gentle blue-green of his eyes changed into severe grey metal discs
of detachment. Either he had no idea how much he'd hurt me or
he genuinely simply didn't give a damn.

I also found it hard to understand my own response when

he started sending me WhatsApps again. All my razor-sharp realisations, all those lessons I should have learned, were soon fading into a slush pile of denial. After just 10 days of IceFreezeYouOutLand, we are chatting again on WhatsApp.

I discovered what a sucker I was for an emoticon. It started with a little shy, blushing face from him. Soon actual words were being exchanged. He revealed he was in a really dark space, a sinking hole of self-deprecation, plummeting downward on some self-hating spiral. But instead a victorious fist-pump that he was suffering, I felt a twinge of compassion, an ache inside, for what he was going through, and before I knew it I'd been pulled in once again. Embarrassing, I know. I am a sponge to pain, that familiar feeling of being hooked in, drawn into the rescue circle. Fuck. How many times have I done this – sublimated my own journey into soreness and, rather than deal with it, tried instead to salvage another? It was all so clear to me, yet I felt powerless to say: "No, fuck off, go and tell someone who gives a damn."

In supreme victim mode, he told me: "You'll be happy to know I've been dumped."

"Told you so," was what I wanted to say, rubbing my hands in glee. "What goes around comes around. The wheel turns. Karma's a bitch" and all the other clichés in the book. But instead I opened up my heart, listened and embraced his pain, and mothered the fuck right out of him again.

When are you going to get it? You can't bury your pain and carry another's, especially when the other is the one hurting you. What's with that insane need to obliterate your own feelings and give another dominion over yours?

I heard the voice clearly, but chose to turn down the volume. Instead, I listened. I received. I advised. I stroked. I mothered. I felt the urge to hold him and love him – and let him suck all the light that I had barely managed to reignite right out of me. Again.

I suggested I could come over and see him later if he liked? Besides, I told him, I needed to give the new Volvo XC60 I was reviewing a ride. He sounded so swollen in his depression, so low, so sad ... my heart was breaking. *Yuck!*

The recall of my own pain was receding faster than Sepp Blatter's hairline. I was forgetting that I was hurt too. Forgetting what had even happened. I was forgetting everything. "Let's make it nice. Let's all make love. Not war. Let's all hold hands and sing a happy hippy song." Although I was sick inside, my codependence swallowed me whole and willed me on.

I had that familiar rush of adrenaline at the idea of seeing him. I even shaved my knees. "You're gonna get laid, baby, or at least get eaten into pussy heaven," whispered the love-sex addict in me.

I received a WhatsApp a few hours later: "I don't think you should come ... I'll just end up fucking you."

Now there's a challenge.

No, motherfucker, I'm coming – I need my fucking fix. The dark addict demon taunted me.

"Don't worry, I won't touch you," I typed back to reassure him, knowing full well I was lying. "I just want to see you, darling. You sound so sad. Besides, I really need my Marianne Williamson book back." Another lame excuse.

A Return to Love. A fat lot of good that's done us ... But, right now, any alibi will do.

Although he didn't sound at all convinced by my reassurances, we agreed to meet later at his place – for "the book", and for some closure. And "no sex", I lied to him. "I promise."

A few hours later we were seated at a table in front of the townhouse he was sharing with a friend. Those face-brick Stepford Wife boxes where everyone looks as though they share the same brain and live on Kellogg's, tartrazine and aspartame.

We relaxed into an easiness of sorts – a lot like old times, actually: witty banter, some serious common thoughts and sharing, even a few tears. Fuck, where am I going to find this kind of easiness on Tinder?

I confessed that I had joined the dating desperadoes, pretended that I'd moved on and that I was glad we were over. It was more important than anything that it looked like my pride had been restored, that he had no inkling of how goddamn much he'd hurt me.

But, inside, it was a hard act to keep up. I could feel it, that I was falling again, down the rabbit hole of twisted love. We decided to go out for pizza and drove off in my diesel Volvo XC60. It felt comfortable. *We* felt comfortable – almost like nothing had happened. But of course there was an elephant in the room, a gorgeous, skinny, red-haired tattooed one, and like some kind of curious "I love pain" sicko I asked: "So … what happened with your new girlfriend?"

My mind was a minefield of flashing images: sucking, fucking, coming … My Clinic Boy, who was so close just last week, was doing exactly what he did to me with another. The notion was driving me crazy. But I'm perverse – I needed to know.

"She's not my girlfriend. I think she despises me."

Oh yeah, right. That self-pitying bullshit again. Yawn.

"Why's that?"

All I was really interested in were the lurid details. Like did he fuck her? Suck her? Eat her? Finger her?

Instead he rambled on about how his attempts to shag her had ended in disaster … Got it up, couldn't keep it up – same old, same old. Let down again by his manhood, which, he told me as we shared a Siciliano pizza, was nonexistent.

Oh god, I was getting so tired of this, this Sad Sack act. Then he revealed how he went down on her instead.

Ahhh … now there was something to hurt myself on. Suddenly all his words were bouncing, rebounding, my outward detachment anything but convincing. My neck. My fucking neck gave it all away. Stretched like a suicide victim atop a skyscraper, hanging from a rope.

"Come, let's go back to your place," I mumbled. "I must get my book back. It's getting late, and I need to sleep."

Back at the townhouse, I decided I wasn't leaving. I told him I was tired, couldn't drive. He looked like a deer caught in headlights. I hated him. What an asshole. Did he have any idea what he was trying so hard to resist?

"Stop being such a baby," I said. "I'll wear clothes. A T-shirt, the one I gave you about being Bipolar. We won't touch each other."

He looked freaked out. Oh god, what a loser.

He couldn't find the T-shirt I had given him so I pulled on one of his other grungy shirts and kept my knickers on. We put out the lights. Within seconds, I was rubbing up against his back. He moved towards the wall, terrified, like I was some kind of a golem. I giggled.

"What's wrong with you, dude? Why don't you just chill the fuck out?" I was getting perverse pleasure out of tormenting him. Within a minute, however, I had what I had come for. He was hard. We fucked. He stayed hard. It wasn't that bad at all. Probably the best sex we had ever actually had because, despite his initial protests, he really got into it. I knew, though, that it would be the last. For some reason, it was important to me that I left him remembering it, wanting more.

The next morning I drove off in triumph, into the savage soup of 7 am highway rush hour. But that bullshit cover-up feeling didn't last long. Soon my face was streaming. It's amazing how many realisations you can come to in the boiling lull of bumper-to-bumper traffic.

There was no denying that my heart had been broken, again, even though I had been pretending I was fine as I swept men left and right on Tinder. My heart had had hardly any time to heal. Yet this time I couldn't just swing a left at the Randburg off-ramp and book into Hotel Hospital. Firstly my medical aid had all but run out, but perhaps most importantly, I realised – for the first time in years – that I needed to allow myself to feel the pain and stay with it. Instead of being held hostage by bottled-up feelings, I had to find a way to feel my anger and tears and let it all out.

Hard and deep and sore as it was, in this pile-up on the highway, as Eddie Vedder launched into "Just Breathe", I found myself weeping, really crying from the bottom of my soul. And I didn't give a fuck whether any of the other highway hostages were watching my meltdown from their metal hearses.

And, as my eyes became more and more swollen and the back up became more and more backed up, a thought swooped down on me in a most unexpected way. Perhaps what upset me most about things ending with Clinic Boy was not that my heart had been trashed or that I had lost mediocre sex or a good conversationist, but rather that I was grieving because I had lost an ending for my book.

Yeah, I know that sounds pretty fucked up, but maybe it was true. I really had fallen in love with the idea of finding love in the Hotel Hospital with a suicidal clinic boy and ending the book with a poetic sunset as we rescue the fuck out of each other. And it was only in the constipated traffic that morning that I realised how sick that sounded.

Sometimes when I look at the pages and pages that make up my existence, and the depths and shallows of my heart, it's easy to be confused between what is driving my life and what is driving my books. But whether my life was feeding my writing or my book was dictating my life, the one thing I did know at that moment, as I sat in this early morning pile-up, was what I was longing for in my life – perhaps more than anything else – was a beautiful relationship with my self. The kind of relationship all the self-help books and Oprah keep telling us about.

And wouldn't it be cool if, once I loved myself, on a deep soul level, I could meet a man to fall in love with, to have a relationship filled with trust and passion and abandon, who would help me break this god-awful pattern I found myself trapped in for what had felt like forever?

Staring at my iPad, as the traffic stood dead still, flicking a few men left, I sure as fuck knew that it wasn't going to happen on Tinder.

And then, just as the cars and trucks began to inch forward, I finally understood – understood that an end of a chapter does not need to be the end of a book.

CHAPTER 24

The Crane

Five days after Clinic Boy and I hooked up for a shag, I was driving past Amuse Café in Linden where there was supposed to be an all-day art market. By this stage, I had swapped my XC60 for the giant Lexus RS Hybrid. I was wearing my purple-flower thrift-shop dress, purple shoes, mauve lips. I knew I looked as beautiful as I could possibly be with the restrictions I carry of not being a pretty girl. I parked. Then, as I neared the outside chill area, I spotted Clinic Boy sitting in the sun with Tattoo Girl. My heart beat like that of a dying pigeon.

I put my brave face on. It was easy to access. I used it most times in my outer world. The steps I took towards him had a strange thud, like the dwarf Tyrion Lannister approaching his heartless father, Tywin.

There were hardly any other people around, but it seemed ridiculous for me not to join them at their otherwise empty table. I greeted. I smiled. I made small talk. I prayed my eyes wouldn't betray me. I laughed. I was struggling to breathe. I turned to her and asked: "Are you in NA too? I am as well."

Clinic Boy had mentioned that she was also in recovery.

"How clean are you?" I said. I couldn't think of anything else. I think she said 20 days … but I couldn't really hear because the blood was pumping so loudly in my brain. In the sunshine, her tattoos bounced off her skin like neon lights dancing off buildings at night.

"That's great – the first 24 hours are the hardest," I babbled. It sounded really dumb, like some line from a cultish sermon. The programme has been so deeply engrained in me that I can recite the druggie drill like a Christian does Psalm 23. "The newcomer is the most important person at a meeting." "You can only keep what you have by giving it away." "Principles before personalities." Blah-di-blah-di-blah.

"And you?" she asked.

"I'm 15 years." I struggled to get it out. Didn't want to look like a know-it-all, all holier than thou, because right then I was feeling all the awkwardness of a mentally and emotionally challenged 15-year-old.

She stood up to hug me. "Let me bow down before you," she grinned.

"Oh no, don't do that," I laughed her off. "I'm probably the most screwed-up person you'll ever meet." Right then I wasn't even joking.

Tattoo Girl was nothing I had hoped. She was nice, sweet. She was a lot like me – bright, chatty, brave. I couldn't help but like her.

All this time, Clinic Boy sat on edge, adding a perfunctory "one day at a time" to the discussion like an empty chapel bell in a Nick Cave song. I turned and glared at him. Motherfucker. But slowly the conversation became less and less awkward. By that point Tattoo Girl and I were getting on like old friends. Clinic Boy was somewhere out there on the plain of the ignored.

She said she needed to get something, and he offered to walk with her. It was clear that his anxiety was mounting, that he needed to get away from me, that he really just wanted me to leave. So I was left alone at the table.

"That dude is a motherfucker," I mutter to no one in particular.

I left soon after.

Later I picked up my friend Hayley. There was a gig at Amuse; a band called To Hire a Nurse, an anarchic trio, were playing. The lead singer, Connor, belted out lines about blow-up girlfriends and dogs dying in their vomit.

I stood alone at the bar inside. A sober freak staring at the shiny bottles as they winked at me. I didn't want to go outside, I didn't want to risk seeing him up close with Tattoo Girl. I had kissed and held him in this place. I couldn't bear to see him looking at another in the way he had looked at me, the way he had touched me on the first night we kissed. Fuck, what was *wrong* with me? He'd told me a hundred times that we should both feel free to frequent the venue. No hard feelings, your friends are my friends blah blah blah … yet I still felt like an imposter.

And then he walked in. It was too late for me to make a getaway – he'd already seen me. He moved closer to buy a drink, his eyes glassy, stoned, semi-psychotic. I tried to adopt my serene Ice Queen stance and sipped demurely on my iced tea. But my anger glinted.

"Hello," I forced a side smile. He looked awkward, like all he wanted to do was run away. I pinned him to the bar with my best stare: Damien from *The Omen*.

"Why d'you look so strange?" I ventured. Smiling. I struggled to turn my "I don't give a fuck" look on with the flick of a switch. I touched his arm. There was pressure in my touch. Perhaps too much.

"Because you look so angry. Please don't touch me."

Touch you? Don't worry, fuckhead, there's no chance of that, I stopped just short of saying.

"Damn right I am." My anger had begun to boil over. My truth spat fire. "I'm pissed off with myself for fucking you Tuesday night, so fucking regretful that I went there … You once said that I wasn't really into mythology. Well, you know what? I actually am and right now I am Medusa with a thousand snakes in my hair."

As inappropriate as ever. This was all sounding like such bullshit. I cringed inside. He tried to look away.

"And, you know what …" There was no stopping me now. "You have been so fucking lucky to have been with a woman like me. I gave you so much love, sex, confidence. I worked so hard on you."

As I said those words, it was so obvious that all that effort was exactly what I did wrong. That that, if anything, was my biggest mistake. Jesus, I wished I could just shut it.

"One thing I can promise you ..." my voice was low and threatening. Now I really was beginning to sound psycho. "You will always think of how much you lost when you decided to fuck with our bond and treat me this way. We both found each other in a clinic. We shared our pain, we put our third eyes against each other. Became a cyclops. We promised we would never cause each other pain. That we would take care of each other's hearts."

"Life is full of pain." He was cold as ice. "Accept it."

"What do you know of pain, little boy? I've been through a thousand miles of pain; I'm the Eiffel Tower of fucking pain. I'm standing at the top, flying with my pain, while you, little motherfucker, you are a little razor blade at the bottom. You haven't even made it to the foot of the first level." I wasn't even sure I was making any sense any more.

Then Tattoo Girl slouched past. She must have seen my eyes flashing at this loser boozer.

"Don't mess with me," I warned, shooting him my best gangster glare. "You know nothing."

Tattoo Girl moved to the door to leave.

"Well, that's all fucked up now," he glared, as he watched her slam the door.

"She must've seen me talking to you. She's leaving. You better go after her," I suggested. But I'm not sure I meant it.

He followed her out and I watched as they exchanged words in a heated flurry of back-and-forths. Then she left without him. And there he stood, all lost, like a little fat boy rejected and abandoned in the playground. I sensed a surge of triumph – he needs to feel rejection, I told myself. He needs to feel it like a thousand knives between the shoulder blades.

"She's left ..." he said as he came back inside. "She wanted me to go to an NA meeting ... but she says I'm drinking and I'm bad for her."

"You probably are," I threw right back at him. I thought of all the cigars I'd smoked since I had met him. You can't blame another person but you can pinpoint triggers. "Anyway, any relationship is going to be bad for her right now," I mutter. "They say that in the

148

first year you shouldn't go for another human being – a pot plant is about as much as you can handle."

He was no longer listening.

"She's rejecting and judging me. Why did you have to come here?"

Boo-hoo! Poor little baby. Feel the pain, motherfucker.

"I'm leaving," he spat and stormed out.

He was back within seconds. I watched him slam through the glass door, stalk in a rage to the bar, and order a beer. Alcohol wins every time. This time there was nothing in me that wanted to reach out to him or hold him and tell him everything will be okay.

I made my way back to Hayley and gave her the blow-by-blow on the events at the bar. She was hardcore. "You fucking leave him alone," she hissed. "He's a mommy's boy and a loser."

I looked at my phone and noticed a really cool little graphic on my Instagram feed, of a girl sitting downcast, sad and forlorn, all in haunting shades of blue. The words read: "The time you confused a lesson for a soul mate." I immediately reposted it on Facebook. I felt better in my barely disguised crypticness, and I hoped he'd read it some day.

I felt the relief that "the final over" offered, the surrender to what was. The much-needed wake-up to truth: it was well and truly over. There was no going back. It took me long enough to get it.

Later, I bought a mounted sketch from the walls of Amuse done by Tattoo Girl. It's called *1000 Cranes*. I was drawn to it; it resonated and bounced straight off the walls at me and even though I knew it was weird to have chosen to buy a piece of art from the girl who had stolen Clinic Boy's heart, it felt like the only thing I could do. A strange peace washed over me as I took it home and leaned it up against my lounge wall.

That night those thousand cranes spoke to me. They told me I needed to reignite my flying self. Slowly I breathed in that realisation. Nothing felt truer to me in that moment.

CHAPTER 25

Getting to Know
Tattoo Girl

The crane is said to a bird capable of flying to the heavens, bearing the spirits of the deceased upon its back. It is seen as a symbol of freedom. It can walk on earth and swim in the sea as humans do, but it also has the ability to soar into the sky. For many cultures, it has come to represent eternal life, the link between heaven and earth, and free to roam between.

The crane also represents maternal love and happiness, a symbol of communication and, some believe, even a messenger of the gods.

Women so often blame the other woman, vilify and trash her. But staring at my beautiful crane sketch, I knew it wasn't Tattoo Girl who had hurt me. She was just the one who released me from my pain, who helped me to lift the veil of truth. She had given me my crane wings, my courage, the momentum to fly. Free to roam the earth and sky. Again and again and again. Maybe this is what they mean by the Christ soul: compassion, truth and the ability to reach through pain. To forgive and transcend the earthly battles we find our human form torn and tethered by.

Sometimes everything seems so big, so dramatic, so crushing in this life that we are completely overwhelmed and lost, like there is no way through. But when I look at the vast expanse of sky at night, the canvas black pricked with little dots of stars, galaxies and entire universes, a million light years away, I know that each human struggle and emotion is just a minuscule pinprick in the bigger scheme of things. Occhiolism – my new favourite word. The awareness of the smallness of your perspective.

But don't misunderstand me. Don't imagine that a bit of grief and heartache have made me go all simpery, New Age and swarmi-ish … you see, a crash of the heart and a car can make you look at the world quite differently. For instance, the Buddha, wise chap that he was, stated that only three things count in the end: how you have loved, how gently you have lived and how gracefully you have to let go of things not good for you. As far as I can see, the first part is a work in progress, in constant reappraisal; the second is something of a failure for me, because "gentle" is not a word anyone has ever used to describe my life. But it is the third part in which I am most interested: the "letting go of things not good for you" part – that's the one I have always found challenging. Because the moment you think too much about it, intellectualise it or try to control it, all you're doing is holding on, tighter than ever. It takes a mammoth non-effort to let go. And as far as the "things not good for you" goes … in my life it's almost been a rule of thumb that those things I struggled most to let go have always been those that have been the worst for me.

It was Monday, 3 November, almost three weeks since Clinic Boy had bust my heart, and two days after I had bumped into him and Tattoo Girl at Amuse. I decided to start the day with the three lessons top of my mind. Spread love. Try to live the day by treating myself and others gently, and let go. It seemed simple enough. 1–2–3, let's go.

151

I also decided to bury the hatchet and sent an upbeat WhatsApp to Clinic Boy, wishing him some happy-day stuff as I sat at my desk, trawling Tinder. When his response pinged, I picked up the phone – a reflex, this phone thing, like reaching out to another limb.

Why the fuck did you come all dressed up like that to Amuse?
Huh? WTF?
You knew I'd be there ... Why did you dress like that? You've never looked so good.

My R8.00 purple thrift-shop dress? Was he for real? I mean, I love that dress, but it was hardly a knockout fuck-me-over-the-table number.

Me: *Are you out of your mind?*

Clinic Boy: *You came there looking like that knowing I would be there with her. You want to fuck up my life. You are evil.*

Jeez. Hello, Monday! While I was conjuring up a sarky reply, I decided to put Lesson 3 into practice, the bit about grace and letting go. But just before I did, the Facebook Messenger alert on my iPad rang. Ping-ring-ping, it was a virtual party of pings. I reached out for my Air, while another stream of WhatsApp whistles vibrated on the other phone.

Gee whizz. It was all coming down.

So what was your poison?

I had to look twice. Was this for real? I read it a third time. Tattoo Girl – on Facebook Messenger.

I stared, shocked. My phone was still whistling – more WhatsApps from Clinic Boy. Oh my god. Surrounded, hemmed in on both sides, like some kind of weird virtual Attack of Social Media. It felt as though the two of them were conspiring against me, and it wasn't even 10 am.

I decided to ignore WhatsApp and turned to Messenger. Poison? Could she mean that purple dress? Bloody hell! It was hardly poison ... Maybe she meant my lipstick – YSL Fiesta matte red. Come to think of it, the lippy could be construed as being on the side of "dangerous", did it really warrant the label "poison"?

When in doubt, act dumb – my go-to mantra.

Me: *Ermmm ... not sure I know exactly what you mean?*

Long pause.

Tattoo Girl: *What led you to NA!*

Ahhh ...

Phew. Relief.

Breathe easy, bitch.

Me: *Oh, drugs! Okay. Heroin, crack ... alcohol ... Everything, really. My drug of choice was More.*

Tattoo Girl: *Ahhh. A menu of poison.*

Me: *Exactly. Anything. Just more more more.*

Tattoo Girl: ☺ *Always. I call it feeding the hole.*

Me: *I started drinking when I was 9.*

Tattoo Girl: *Me 13.*

Me: *It's the black pit. The hole in the soul.*

Tattoo Girl: *The more you feed it the hungrier it gets.*

Me: *The vacuum. Jung called it a "spiritual thirst". I call it a monster.*

Tattoo Girl: *Haha. Exactly my words.*

Me: *You are a lot like me.*

Bloody hell. A twin.

I was at my desk, transfixed by the words Tattoo Girl was typing. Pulled in, as I typed mine back to her.

Tattoo Girl: *Yes, I sensed that. And now? How does it work?*

Me: *Some days are easy. Right now I am struggling a lot.*

A lot. That was an understatement. I had been crying for three weeks. Barely able to come up to gulp for air.

A long wait. Then Tattoo Girl was back.

Tattoo Girl: *I sense everything I need to know in seconds. It's the side effect of anxiety.*

Me: *Me too. A walking litmus paper. The civilised way of describing it is "an empath", otherwise known as a fucking boundary-less sponge.*

Tattoo Girl: *Yes. I am an emotional idiot.*

Me: *Me too. Welcome to my world* ☺

Tattoo Girl: *A child.*

Me: *I am 4 years old. A little skinned baby.*

Tattoo Girl: *I've suppressed/drugged/drowned – every emotion born.*

Me: *Me too*

Then it tumbled out that I had bought her *1000 Cranes*. Typing the words felt almost like a confession.

Tattoo Girl: *No way.*

I could sense her genuine surprise over the miles and miles of electric signals that connected our hearts.

Me: *It's beautiful. It spoke to my soul.*

Tattoo Girl: *Do you know the story? A thousand cranes is a wish. The Japanese fold paper cranes for weddings and things.*

Me: *I know they are meant to be the gateway between heaven and earth.*

Tattoo Girl: *When the bomb dropped on Nagasaki, a girl lay dying. The doctors told her that to live she had to fold a thousand cranes from medical papers to keep her busy. Although she died, she still became a symbol of hope. That's why I have my crane tattoo. Wait, let me send it to you.*

I was in awe, struck by the connectedness of things. That I had taken a risk, bought the *1000 Cranes*, and now both Tattoo Girl and cranes had manifested for me. I felt as though I had folded my thousand papers and my Crane had come alive. While she was looking for her crane tattoo, I continued to type.

Me: *I love that I bought your drawing. It spoke a thousand things to me. Flying into the unknown. Out of grief, with hope on my wings.*

There was a long, connected pause, and the image appeared on my screen.

Tattoo Girl: *What is the pain in your words?*

I was caught off guard. Instinctively, I knew she meant Clinic Boy – her new boy, my ex-boy, whose residue of pain I carried with me inside like a little box of ashes.

I changed the subject.

Me: *Bad week. My friend Kelly has gone through lots of stuff. Her boyfriend Senzo, the goalkeeper, you know … He got shot – you know, all that horrendous pain. It's consumed me.*

I am hopeless at deflecting and I could tell that this strange Russian girl, storyteller of cranes and covered in ink, knew my truth. I felt like I knew her, yet I knew nothing at all: what her motives were in befriending me, why she was making small talk about weddings and birds, coming out of nowhere like a feather dropping from the sky, swooping in and delving into my pain.

And she didn't let up. Later, as I scoured the typed lines for clues, I came to believe that what she asked next was what she had really come for.

Tattoo Girl: *Okay, another question if I may be direct.*

Then the image I had posted onto my Instagram wall at Amuse at 8 pm Saturday night appeared.

It was the one that showed the back of a sad girl huddled in a grey bath with the words: *The time you confused a lesson for a soul mate.*

Tattoo Girl: *Did this happen? Linden 8 pm?*

Me: *Err … hang on, I am not sure what you are meaning ?*

Tattoo Girl: *Am I right in thinking I understand this?*

Me: *Ask me directly.*

Of course I knew what she meant. I was just forcing her hand.

Tattoo Girl: *Is he the pain?*

Me: *Of course.*

I breathed in. Slow. My virtual voice just a whisper. It was so fragile … the font echoing a thousand shattered pieces.

Me: *Definitely.*

Tattoo Girl: *Do you love him?*

Wow. I was not prepared for that. Love him? How could I answer that? I hated him right then, that's for sure. Did I love him? Love? Damn right if post-clinic rebound love counts – it certainly felt like it did at the time. Finally, I managed a few words, but they were hard to get out. Like when the Little Mermaid must walk on sharp stones for the first time after she has swapped her tail for feet.

Me: *I thought I did. But I don't any more.*

It sounded like the lyrics from a Gotye song. "Somebody that I used to know."

There ... it was out. Now I wanted to bolt, run, be like that paper crane and fly away.

Tattoo Girl: *I need to know. I am sorry but I have to ask you.*

She sounded desperate. In some kind of pain too.

I decided to take the truth plunge with her. I liked her. I didn't even know her, but I liked her. Plus, I had her drawing in my lounge. It didn't feel like she was going away.

Now that he was on the table and small talk had all but evaporated, it was amazing how quickly we unravelled his lies and betrayal. We hauled out our virtual calendars, my iPad having kept track of my life. We started talking dates. We began to join the dots.

Discrepancies began to emerge. We started firing the all-revealing questions. Two women on the hunt to decimate a man who had betrayed us.

When was the first time you slept with him?

Were you with him last Thursday?

Did he ever mention me?

When did he say he met me?

The details, his lies, the shadiness of his actions – they all began to paint an uncannily bleak picture, one we had both been suspecting but had no ammo to confirm.

Two women lied to. Two women enraged. How many times have two women both known they have been played? And what are the chances of them ever actually getting together at one table and working in tandem to establish the truth?

Us comparing notes went on for hours. And on that first day our bond was carved out. Like a newly inked bird on the third eye. It was clear we were on a mission to get to the bottom of the lies we had both been fed.

By the time we finished, it was time to drive home through the Sandton gridlock, the traffic jungle.

I don't want a relationship that's born on another woman's grave.

That was her parting shot.

* * *

A friendship blossomed between us. Its seeds sprung from a virtual inquisition. It was weird – something I had never experienced. Women usually stalk each other in shrouds of daggers. They hardly ever open up and make themselves known as they scratch and dig into the scars that refuse to grow skin. They are more likely to drive themselves demented, in the hidden psycho shame of searching for photos on social networks, meanings and clues to expose the horrible truth that their lovers' hearts are just shallow tin things. They would rather do that than look each other in the eye and seek the truth.

In most cases, instead of joining forces with the other woman – who is being lied to just as much as they have been – they approach the invader as an enemy, blame her and make her the epicentre of their heartache. But what they usually never do is show themselves in the light and work together.

Tattoo Girl's straightforward approach had left me disoriented but intrigued. It may have had something to do with the fact that she is Russian. The offspring of Chekhov, Lenin and Nabokov. There were no frills, no sweet little whispers in her approach. She was a master of getting to the truth, hitting the ache right on the button. I began to refer to her as "my little KGB".

We found ourselves chatting every day, sometimes for hours, typing away into each other's hearts. Even though Clinic Boy had been the initial gelling point, we found ourselves establishing a new connection, moving away from referencing him at every turn. There were many ideas exchanged, and sometimes we even forgot the outrage that had brought us together. Our sharing became deeper. We were beginning to carve something more than the sum of two women scorned.

And, although we were two women kindling the flames of friendship on the grave of an ex-lover, we soon found out that we really liked each other. Full stop.

We decided to meet at an NA meeting and go out for coffee afterwards. I arrived just after the meeting had started. I immediately caught sight of her Mercurochrome-red hair and twig-like tattooed arms. There was an empty chair beside her. We sat next to each other, two sisters of sobriety who had been scorned.

Those harsh lights so often used in church or school halls, where most meetings take place, left nothing unexposed. As the preambles to the meeting were read, and people took turns to introduce themselves around the circle, I could almost feel our hearts beat in unison.

Afterwards we made our way to a coffee shop on Grant Avenue. It was a grimy Monday night in Norwood, not much life on the street. We found a table in a quiet, dimly lit space in the rooftop bar area where we could both smoke. I was still telling myself that I was "relapsing on cigars", but in reality at this stage I was simply smoking. There is no other honest way to say it. It's incredible how quickly and easily you move from the Non-smoking section to Smoking. We shared a plate of mixed Middle Eastern meze and spent the next few hours talking about life, books and words,

She told me a story about her grandmother who fell in love with a beautiful man, a poet, who made her heart soar and sing. She gave her very best years to him – her looks, her love, her body.

Then one day he wrote a poem about how her beauty had cracked into old. How the grapes of her breasts had turned to bunches of hanging garlic. The poem all but destroyed her. His words carved knives into her heart and she never recovered. She grew old and alone, hardly ever getting out of bed to face the world. Not able to look in the mirror again, she pined away in solitary self-shame.

"A man did that to her," Tattoo Girl looked across at me. Her Russian accent was strong, her big eyes flashed with rage and penetrated my soul. Her tattoos gleamed, even in the dark. The recent one, *Just for Today*, she had just had inked, scabs still red around the edges. I really wanted to get a tattoo.

"It could happen to anyone, what happened to my grandmother. We can't ever let that happen to us." She stared intently at me, forcing me to agree. I did.

She came with some deep wisdom, did Tattoo Girl. I could see why Clinic Boy had unplugged me in exchange for her. That was a big one for me. It cut deep into my primal wound – the one of rejection and abandonment – but somehow, with her, I was in some crazy way relieved that it was for this girl and not some airhead Barbie doll that I had been replaced. But rejection will always hurt like those scabs on her forearm, so I tried to channel the Buddha for a second: let go of that which is bad for you.

Finally, the conversation turned to him, to our Clinic Boy. He had been hanging around like a big, pink elephant in the room. She had many questions. I watched her carefully as she latched onto the information I fed her, processing and packaging it like a meat packer in some icy Moscow factory. I could see by her hunger, by the questions she asked and by the expression in her eyes, as she consumed my words, that she was not entirely ready to let go of him. She cared too much for the answers I brought, the anger I shared, the recollections, the memories, the lies he had fed us both. We both cared too much.

I was conflicted. I realised, too, that I may have been giving her food to fuel her desire of him. But, as Kundera said in *The Unbearable Lightness of Being*, "*Es muss sein.*" It must be. Everything about us, our meeting, our connection to Clinic Boy, all the truths that were unravelling, felt like fate, as if we had no choice. It was all just part of the bigger picture.

Nietzsche, who had significant influence on Milan Kundera, spoke about the concept of eternal return and how we could embrace this idea and love the burden that comes with it – in other words, love one's fate. That is how we make peace with our decisions and ultimately the tapestry of our lives.

I, however, ached from the repercussions of our connection and yet, all at once, I was relieved and even felt a whisper of gratitude. It was a seesaw – the dark, the light, the love, the hate, the black and white of a person's soul.

Then we got talking about the sex. This part of the conversation held all the juiciness. A few minutes previously, we had been dark and sad, like two twisted sisters in a mad Russian drama, mourning Moscow. Then, suddenly, we are both bright-eyed and alert. Surged with sapiosexual energy. There is something deliciously dirty when two women congregate to compare notes on their sexual experiences. Tattoo Girl and I spared no details.

After some extremely detailed comparisons, we both agreed that we had had to work far too hard on him. I told her that I was genuinely relieved I would no longer have to play the rather boring role of sex therapist.

As the night grew older and longer, so this strange connection with this tiny Russian girl grew stronger. We both sensed that Clinic Boy was just the glue that had brought us together, and that something much bigger was happening here. A blue-black crow and a heaven-bound crane nestled between us; birds of a feather, from the underworld, had come to shift our worlds.

And although two women getting together to talk about men can become a funeral pyre of dissing, it can also become ever-multiplying banners of wisdom, unfurling across the ink-black Milky Way, the star-dotted sky.

Just before we got up to leave, and as hard as it was, I reminded her of his other parts – his beautiful side, the long talks we shared, his soft eyes, how more than anything he was the best listener and guardian of conversations.

I ended off by saying: "We all make mistakes. We all tell lies, both to ourselves and others. Who am I to judge him for the untruths he has told? We can all change. We all have the chance to recover."

I had the sense that the last of my words would help her decide. I knew she would go back to him. Even if it was just for a bit to find out more about why she should leave. I was clearly handing the choice back to her.

And so we parted ways as the black night sucked us into our cars and we drove back to our own worlds. It was strange to feel so free and yet, simultaneously, to feel so lost and empty.

Over the following week, I stood back from the love triangle. It felt weird that I liked her, really liked her. But what was even weirder was that I no longer felt as much hatred for him either.

Somewhere, on a far-off recovery horizon, I had the sense that he had come into my life as some kind of a reprieve from pain, a gift the universe delivered to soften the hard fall after Ex-Boyfriend.

Perhaps it was that 15 years of walking through the fires of sobriety had given me certain skills to cope. Instead of wallowing in the darkness of hatred, blame and self pity, I tried to force myself to think of the good stuff: how, for five healing months, we spent almost every single day touching each other's hearts. Connecting and smiling and spreading the love. So, instead of falling into the trap of hate, I worked hard on finding the lesson – even though it would have been far easier to hate him. And sometimes I still do.

"What you resist persists," so the saying goes. And so the opposite must hold true too: "What you release diminishes." By trying to forgive what had hurt me, I began to feel a slow sense of letting go. It was tiny, and sometimes it wanted to hold on, to stick, struggle, and claw at me; it tried to devour me, but when I did manage to let go, slowly it faded away, even if it was just a little drip-drop-drip-drop at a time.

And, in the end, surrender comes with deep relief.

CHAPTER 26

CTRL. ALT.
DELETE.

Okay, good, you may sigh. At least this book is not going to be one of those happy-ending fairy tales in which the chick and dude waltz into the sunset, hand in hand, the scene dripping in cheese as the credits roll. But don't think I haven't been searching for and constructing the perfect ending for months. Tearing into my timeline to hunt down Price Charming, that rose-tinted relationship that will put all my pain, all my empty ache to bed and leave me with the last few pages of a book in which you will all look at my life, amazed, in awe ... dumbstruck, hashtag #OMG #YOLO #Wtf in wanting my #brilliant and #fabulous #hashtag #Life.

Don't think I haven't been slaving away to get all the pieces of my life tied up together and neatly packaged in a Christmas biscuit tin with cute, furry-purry kittens, adorned in a flurry of pastel pink-and-blue ribbons, in order to pen the perfect ending.

Because, despite me appearing to be a hardcore highwayman in black, a Nick Cave ex-junkie queen, the oblivion chaser who trainspotted the road of smack and crack, at the core of me I really am a softie, a girl who longs for the superimposed time-lapsing sunset.

I have spent years searching for perfection, bombarding my timeline with a soft-focus life, a life where the blur between fantasy and reality is indistinguishable. Mine is a Facebook-timeline-motherfucking life, made up of photographs and postings of my perfect adventure-filled, never-a-dull-moment-in-Mel's-world existence: all those Great Wall of China selfies, lamb vindaloo close-ups in Goa, white-sand moments on Sugar Beach, smog and symmetry in Shanghai; shiny new Jaguars, Porsches, Bentleys, turbo-charged RSs; the life of a glam rock-star motor-journalist writer. It is a life that sees me changing my profile pic at least once a week, sometimes once a day, making sure it's always the best angle, corrected with veneers of Ludwig or Early Morning. Or tapping on the Beauty Face option on my cellphone to make sure there are not too many give-away crinkles to show.

The more stimuli I gather from without, the more paintings and photos and quotes from The Mind Unleashed and Brain Pickings I find to impress and fill my timeline, the more I hope I will feel. So I post, post, post, like some manic wasp at a shrouded window, waiting for the ping of a Like. Desperate to be delivered from the invisible, from the god-awful anonymity of a pre-Facebook world, from a time before the Big Matrix sucked us in and made Timeline Vampires of us all. And yet, despite my "Zuckerberg says you cannot accept any more" 5 000 Facebook friends, with 2 345 waiting for approval, despite the 6 000 following me on Twitter, the 1 500 on Insta, despite this rugby field of people who like and approve of me, why do I sometimes just feel so goddamn fucking alone and empty? Why do I, when I look at this life I have created, feel so hollow and scared sometimes? No wonder I'm seduced by the idea of a perfect life – because I am a fool for the theatre of the unreal.

Within weeks of the end of Clinic Boy, I discover one day that he has deleted me as a Facebook friend. I'm astonished at how real it feels when someone detonates you.

Control. Alt. Delete. That's how we roll these days. When something gets too much, when it gets too real, when a truth bashes through the screen like the errant glove of a boxing champ, we click the cursor on *Delete*, press the *End call* button. It's the quick fix, quick unfix, quick-fix-quick-unfix. Ctrl.Alt.Delete ... the cancer of our age.

That's the nature of relationships conducted on the Net, across billions of wires and signals, in the doctored, made-up nirvana world of Facebook, Instagram and Pinterest, where we play out our perfectly filtered and saturated lives, sharpened and deflawed, so that everyone can see just what a wonderful existence we own.

We don't talk about those moments when we collapse, small and crumpled like a battered R10 note. The moments when the emptiness swallows us up as we confront the cracks that connect our small and pitiful lives. When we wake up red-eyed from weeping songs in dreams that remind us that there was once more to it all than this. Instead, we post last night's dinner on Instagram, that sunset we distracted ourselves with as a woman lay dead and bleeding with her legs wrapped around her neck, blood spread like roadkill in a hit-and-run on William Nicol. Twisted Barbie. Even a rotting corpse can have a certain charm when its filtered with Nashville, Early Bird, X Pro2, Ludwig or Valencia.

* * *

And so it was that I used that post-relationship emptiness and loss as a catalyst to establish new habits. After Clinic Boy and I crash, I am forced to take a deep, hard look at my life and realise that I have been in non-ending relationships with men since I was 16. That's almost three decades of serial relationships, with give or take a few months in between. Ever since I started dating, my relationships have overlapped with each other, like the layers on a Japanese fashion sandwich.

All my adult life, I have basically followed the ways of a world that told me that being in a relationship will give me inner meaning and a sense of belonging.

One day when I am very old and look back on my days, I hope to call some of those years my Serial Killer of Self period. Because what comes often with a relationship, at least in my books, is a giving up of self. At 17, I drank Castle because my boyfriend did, and changed to Amstel with the new one. I smoked heroin the first time because the man who would become my husband looked handsome when he chased the dragon. I grew my hair for another and cut it off for the next. I broke my lungs on crack for seven years because I had seen it in the movies. I even went gangsta when my Mitchell's Plain lover got me to explore, like Braille, the machete scars on his head.

"You have an Electra complex," my therapist, Tine, tells me during one of my post-Clinic Boy sessions. An Electra complex? At least it *sounds* all Greek and tragic, much better than "Bipolar" or "Hypomanic" or "Clinically Depressed". But although I have heard about Electra and Clytemnestra and Agamemnon, Euripides and Aeschylus, I am not really sure what this new label actually means. And, of course, when you're unsure of anything, there is no better oracle to consult than God Google.

The Electra Complex, coined by Carl Jung, is essentially a psychoanalytical term used to describe a girl's sense of competition with her mother for the affections of her father. It is pretty much the female equivalent to the Oedipus Complex, embodying the female child's erotic desire for the father and her simultaneous fear of her mother, who is her competitor.

But what happens when your father keels over in front of you and takes his last breath as you, just four years old, watch helplessly, witness the man you adore die? How does the equation of the Electra Complex apply to you then?

I look at the patterns in my affairs of the heart and realise that, perhaps as a result of my father dying in the way he did, I develop a deep adoration, an almost "fetishisation", of men in general. I am cursed with a kind of cock-blindness when it comes down to being able to discern between the Goodies and the Baddies. Just having a dick, a male identity, gives them cred; hence my often indiscriminate god-awful taste in them. And hence my deep love and loathing for them.

This all suddenly begins to make some magical sense. I finally

165

start to understand my at-times obsessive fascination with Sylvia Plath's seminal poem "Daddy", which I have carried around like some inner prayer, some mantra, ever since I stumbled upon it in the *Colossus* collection in the local library when I was just 10 years old. "Daddy" has been analysed to death by scholars as an example of Plath's Electra Complex. Little Sylvia too saw her father, Otto Plath, keel over and die when she was just eight years old, which left profound scars on her psyche. She would subsequently write how she had to figuratively kill "Daddy", how he died, "marble heavy", before she had "time". While I had been trying for most of my adult life to kill my mother, my perceived Electra competitor for my father's love, perhaps it was Daddy I should have been after.

It's time I do something about this fallout that's been torturing me for over four decades. And so, five months after leaving the clinic, I finally do what the therapists told me I needed to do when I got there: I decide I truly have to be alone. Since Hotel Hospital, I have hardly shed a tear about Ex-Boyfriend – instead, I latched onto Clinic Boy, who immediately became my saline plug. My distraction.

Now I need to get real and cry about what's really hurt me, unravel my long journey into self-harm and try to understand where it began and how I can heal it.

CHAPTER 27

Bikram

Now when a girl needs to be all internal and Greta Garbo, there is no better place to meet the soul, mind and heart than in a 40-degree heated Bikram yoga room, where sweating and crying go hand in hand with breathing.

I had been to my first Bikram class about four years previously and, for almost 18 months, went religiously four to five days a week. What I didn't realise back then, however, was how absolutely vital it is to rehydrate and take mineral supplements. Within a year, I was wilting like wax. Instead of enjoying the many benefits – increased flexibility and fitness, mindfulness, self-discipline, focus and willpower – I was experiencing the real contraindications: heat exhaustion, sporadic muscle cramps, light-headedness, dizziness, and a feeling of being physically wiped out.

At the time, I found myself coming home after a 90-minute class and nodding off on Ex-Boyfriend's couch within 30 minutes of saying hello, without even eating dinner. One day I decided I was just too exhausted to go to a class. And I never went back.

Around this time, in 2013, some really worrying things were being published around the yoga's founder, the somewhat eccentric and controversial multimillionaire, Bikram Choudhury. A number of women had come forward with sexual harassment suits; others who claimed that Bikram, who is known for prancing around the studios of his teacher training classes in leopard-print Speedos, had sexually assaulted them. Others believed he had taken the entire thing too far, imagining himself as the untouchable leader of a cult that now boasted over 1 700 studios worldwide, with more than two million yogis being instructed by 8 000 officially trained teachers.

Look, it's easy to think that the practice is a little weird. We do look a bit like a bunch of A-type Moonies sometimes, dressed in skimpy sweat-drenched outfits and armed with rehydrate and water. But none of the rumours or accusations levelled at Choudhury have ever deterred me from my practice. It's easy to dismiss an entire religion or, in this case, an exercise regime because of its founder, but it seems ludicrous to me not to participate in a form of exercise because the founder, who most of us have never actually met, has been accused of wrongdoing. It's like refusing to ever eat bread or drive an Audi again because a baker or car engineer was once accused of murdering his wife.

So, undeterred by negative press, I eventually found myself back in a Bikram class, trying to lick my wounds and mend a heart that had been broken too many times. Armed with my solo status, mat, towel, water and rehydrate, I began my new journey, but this time I made a vow to myself to do it properly – drink loads of water and supplement properly.

There is nothing quite like shedding layers of tears in a sauna-like environment, while contorting into extreme yoga positions, where weeping and sweating become one and the same thing. And no one even knows you're crying.

At 5:30 one morning in November 2014, in the middle of a 40-degree-hot yoga class, sweat dripping, I find myself in the restorative pose or *savasana*, having just completed two rounds of the excruciating back-bend-like deep inversion Camel Pose, otherwise known as *ustrasana*. Basically the Camel posture is part of the floor series and is one of the last in the 90-minute session. By this stage of the class one is usually drenched in sweat, stamina stretched to the limits. One of the deepest back bends in Bikram, the Camel creates maximum compression of the spine, which stimulates the nervous system. Because Camel hits straight at the heart chakra, the *anahatra*, the impact the posture has on the spirit is enormous and I finally come to terms with how broken my poor heart is.

Something amazing happens as I – in unison with the rest of the class – slowly place my hands on my lower back, carefully tilting my head backwards so I can see the wall behind me, and then allow gravity to take over, lifting my chest as high as I can, while pushing the rest of my body forward. I become very aware of the organ that beats deep within – a warm centre that is alive and enormous. And my heart speaks as I see fragments of my life flash before me ...

The years of self-inflicted abuse, crack pipes sucked so deep that my lungs bleed, making my heart speed until it almost cracks out of my ribs, then thick wads of sulky heroin, tar slowing it down to an almost imperceptible, standstill beat. Thousands of cigarettes and now cigars coating my poor lungs black, constricting the veins from my heart, thwarting the mission to take the blood to all the pit stops in my body. Loving people who couldn't love me back, breaking my silly trusting heart over and over again – pain, abuse, cruelty ...

Immediately, as I come out of the posture and lie back on my mat in the *savasana*, the enormity of it all almost drowns me. The tears flow free; they will not stop. Mixed with sweat, mixed with blood, mixed with more tears, there is no end to it. It's as if my heart walls have burst, as if its shell, which has been fossilised for so long, has finally broken open. And I am suddenly filled with such gratitude. Because I know that somehow, within the core of my broken heart, no matter how sore it is right now, lies my strength and my radar for understanding and feeling compassion. My heart is me.

And then, as I become aware of the beat of it thudding in perfect metronomic time, in the silent, humid 40-degree Bikram room, echoing across the whole of the still sleeping city, still shrouded in Bible black, I make a deep and profound realisation: The greatest harm I have inflicted on anyone on my long and jagged life's journey is on myself. That, despite all the amends I have tried to make over the years to everyone I stole from, lied and cheated, the person I have most damaged is me.

"That I feed the hungry, forgive an insult, and love my enemy ... all these are undoubtedly great virtues," said Carl Jung "But what if I should discover that the poorest of beggars, the most impudent of offenders ... are within me, and that I stand in need of the alms of my own kindness – that I myself am the enemy who must be loved – what then?"

What then indeed. What then?

These words are profound to me, almost biblical. Unpacking their meaning may be the greatest realisation I have ever made on my journey of healing. Discovering that I, me, myself have been my own worst enemy. I am the one who has broken my heart, the one who has tightly held the knife and cut the deepest. It is me who leaps into the hottest fire without looking, me who runs over the burning embers, and me who embarks without fail on the bloodiest path.

I am momentarily defeated by this realisation. It rocks my perception of myself in my world. But I have no choice but to breathe and open the door to the next room of my battered soul. And it is in this ache of self-awareness that I am given the gift of realisation around my smoking.

Up until now, all through this time, I have continued to swallow the smoke of cigars as if they are the last drops of water on earth. What started off as a few puffs at a rock fest in August has continued to balloon into a three-month habit of five to 10 cigars a day. It's now early November. Lying in my tear-soaked *savasana*, the true insanity of it all cracks open. The madness of leaving a Bikram class, detoxed and glowing, only to light up in the car, is like kicking all the self-love and nurturing to the pavement. In the heated studio I feel the ground along every millimetre of my body and breathe deep and long and slow to the very bottom of my soul.

I give myself space for an *a-ha* moment, for that truth to come rolling in. I see the mockery of it all with each puff I have ever taken.

And then it dawns in me. All this time, since the day I picked up when I was 16, with each drag and pull I have ever taken of a cigarette or cigar, all I have really been wanting to do is to breathe. Breathe. Sip up oxygen from the huge cup of life. Breathe.

In that moment I know that it's over. I know it. The smoking. *All I have ever wanted to do was breathe.* I say it over and over to myself. I never have to smoke again. All I have ever wanted to do was breathe. Perhaps it's not so much my broken heart that needs fixing. Perhaps love starts in my lungs. I never have to read that book again, never have to go to a Smoke-Enders meeting, never have to tell myself to stop. Because deep inside, I have turned the switch off. I've surrendered. It's already over. All I have ever wanted to do was breathe.

I leave the class, chuck away the five-pack of cherry-tipped cigars I have stashed in the cubbyhole, and don't smoke again.

With newfound clarity, I decide to stop paying ridiculous amounts of money for one-on-one therapy. I have been in and out of therapy for years and suddenly I feel like it's enough. I am tired of spending R800 an hour in a therapist's office, talking and talking, going over my life, round and round in circles, in words-words-words, and never really feeling like I'm healing from within.

Now Bikram becomes my therapist. The extreme nature of the 90-minute heated classes, the 26 postures that challenge every cell of my being, are teaching me inner resilience and fortitude. Each time I don't give up, and see a back bend, a forward bend, a hamstring ache through, my body teaches my emotional centre to not be afraid. To feel it, see a thought, and feel right through to the bitter achy end. I am learning to stop avoiding.

Self-love is a big one. I can no longer avoid the idea that I will never find real love with someone else until I can find it in my heart to love myself. Bikram becomes my self-reflecting therapy. Day in and day out, I am forced to see my outsides in the mirrors that surround me, while I am inspired to look within. There is no escape. I just have to pitch up and keep on going back to see my fears and hopes and truths revealed. Little by little by little, day by day, the shifts that can move mountains in the mind and heart are taking place.

CHAPTER 28

Breaking Out

I think everything in life amounts to experience. And yet, when I
look at my life, the cliché "once bitten twice shy" has never really
applied to me. I mean, you would have thought that after escaping
the deathly clutches of a heroin and crack cocaine near-death
addiction that I would never have allowed myself to slip back into
the clutches of toxic relationships and machine enslavement. But
I have. And just as I should have walked away from my nine-
year relationship much earlier, I should also have left my job at
The Magazine years before I did. But I guess, like the bruised
and battered woman who stays in her marriage, frozen by fear,
sometimes the longer you stay in a job, no matter how untenable
the circumstances become, the harder it is to leave.

On 2 December 2014, a week before the conditions of my
year-long disciplinary "Ferrari Final Written Warning" expire,
I am informed that I am to appear before another disciplinary
committee. I am notified on a Friday afternoon as I'm about to
leave the office, by way of an email from the HR woman who has
been watching me closely ever since I got the Ferrari "Get Out of
Jail Free" card. I happen to walk into her office one day and I see
that she has entire files compiled on me.

"You really take your job seriously," I tell her one day, half
jokingly. "Your nickname could be Nancy Drew."

The new email is headed: *Kelly Khumalo*.

Fucking hell. My head goes into a panicked whirr, my heart beating three million strokes per second. It always does that when authority sniffs me out.

Of course, I know precisely what it refers to. I have written a story for a Sunday newspaper within the group, the same company that owns the magazine I work for. The story in question centres around Kelly Khumalo's devastating loss when her boyfriend Senzo Meyiwa – captain of Bafana Bafana – was gunned down at her mother's home in Vosloorus.

Having written her biography back in 2012, I consider Kelly more of a friend than just a pop-star acquaintance, so when I hear of the devastating news and that she wants to see me, I drop everything, ask my magazine editor for permission to leave work early and fly off to console the grieving singer.

A day later the editor of the newspaper calls to ask me to write an opinion piece on Kelly. She is unaware that I have actually seen Kelly in person, she is hoping that I can write something based on the fact that I have got to know Kelly on an intimate level, as her biographer.

I embrace the task. The writing flows like warm honey and for the next two hours I get lost in the recall of the visit to the embattled singer. Now this, my story, has landed me in hot water:

Late on Tuesday afternoon, I drive through a boiling cauldron of rush-hour traffic to Kelly Khumalo's home in the south of Johannesburg.

I have no idea where we're going. I'm with Percy, Kelly's friend, who's told me that Kelly wants to see me. I cried when he called me.

I have heard from Percy that Kelly has fled her mother's home in Vosloorus, the tiny house where, two days earlier, her goalkeeper boyfriend, South Africa's soccer hope and dream, Senzo Meyiwa, was brutally shot by alleged robbers.

One of three bullets exploded into his back and heart in front of seven people – including Kelly; her mother, Ntombi; her sister,

Zandile; and Christian, her six-year-old son, whom she conceived with convicted killer Molemo "Jub Jub" Maarohanye.

Like rabid rats, the media, shoving cameras and note pads into her tear-soaked face, have put paid to her returning to the little matchbox home. She has fled like a woman sentenced to be stoned at dawn.

The public crucifixion of Kelly during this time of grief has left me revolted and reeling. She's been vilified on social media, called "bitch", "whore" and "murderer", accused of causing Senzo's death by vicious virtual vampires who shoot bullets like cowards in the back. They call for judgment and retribution, they declare a competition of grief between wife and mistress. Kelly is always on the losing side.

I pray she hasn't scrolled through any of the frenzied hate-infested timelines that stretch for miles. I am mostly disgusted by how most of the cruelty is meted out by women. I fear that if she has read any of the vitriolic threads, she will be sent right over the edge, plummeting into a dark space of no return. I turn away from Twitter and Facebook, disgusted by humanity. The focus has shifted from the senseless killing of our national captain to a Day of Judgment on the Internet.

From the moment the news of the brutal shooting breaks, I obsess about how much fear and blood and chaos there must have been that night. I can't stop thinking about it.

I spent time in that home, while writing my book The Kelly Khumalo Story two years earlier. The house, with SPAZA spray painted on the front wall, is tiny; the huge television and couch take up most of the living room. The kitchen where the two killers burst through is even smaller.

The sun is losing shine as we arrive at Kelly's hideout; a face-brick gated complex. A car packed with media, with the eyes of vigilantes, is parked outside.

I am afraid to see Kelly. What am I going to say to her?

Will I be able to hold her, receive her pain, tell her some empty words like: this too shall pass, that it will all be okay, when I see her?

I first met Kelly Khumalo in an empty restaurant in Norwood one stormy night in October 2012. The ink-black sky was electric, thunder and lightning cracked like some prescient omen as I walked towards a table where Kelly and Sarah, her manager at the time, sat like two lost souls. She was much tinier in real life, out of the tabloids.

Over the last few years we'd all become sick of the sensational headlines. Of fallouts with managers, legal battles, of cat fights with Khanyi Mbau. The recent images of Kelly, weave messed up, swollen-lipped, bruised black and blue, had snuffed out our memories of the once young nubile Zulu singing sensation who had burst onto the music scene with her mega hit "Qinisela".

As I neared her [at that first meeting], I first noticed her expensive snakeskin boots. And then I saw her face. A freshly made scar, the size of a 5-cent piece, aching to heal, dug into her skin just above the jawline. She would later tell me that this was where Jub Jub bit her during a last round of fights. It was one of many of life's war wounds she carried. Growing up in Ntinini in rural northern KwaZulu-Natal, she had fought tooth and nail for a chicken foot at Christmas, for her survival.

She'd recently left the cocaine and alcohol-fuelled relationship behind. I was shocked by how wasted her unmade-up dull eyes and face looked.

But as much as I was repelled by what I saw, I took her to her first Narcotics Anonymous meeting that night. Her desperation was clear. She was ready to receive help.

I grew to know and love her tenacious, streetwise spirit and child-like heart. We began to work on her biography, and a firm friendship was cemented.

And now, as I approach the door of the home where she is hiding, I find myself reaching out to God. Not one to pray a lot, I ask for guidance, for strength to hold and receive her pain.

I walk into a lounge tinged with grief. Images of Senzo in action are everywhere; among them photos of the two so obviously in love.

I have hardly followed their love affair – the tabloids and weeklies repelling me with garish lines on cat fights, lies, make-ups and break-ups. I can't keep track of the love triangle: of how the couple are on again, off again, like some indecisive flickering light switch. I don't want to – it all seems so intrusive and callous.

But sometimes the bold letters that scream from the covers of weekly magazines and Sunday tabloids are unavoidable. The one headline that seems consistent is that Kelly is always branded the home wrecker while Mandisa gets the faithful and long-suffering wife treatment. It is only when I hear on the radio, driving to work one morning in October 2013, that Kelly's been arrested for assault for an incident that took place in August, during which a highway clash with Senzo's wife Mandisa erupted, that I really tune in to listen. I am immediately worried. Has Kelly resorted to old behaviour – I feel like I have lost touch with her, let her down since the book, and now things are falling apart. I castigate myself. What kind of a friend am I? I make a mental note to call her. I forget.

A month later I reluctantly pick up Drum *magazine and read how, after appearing at the Hillbrow Magistrate's Court, the charges of assault and malicious damage to property are dropped. It seems Senzo has made a statement to police in defence of Kelly, that it was in fact his wife Mandisa who had tried to sandwich her between their two cars as they drove on the highway south. I read the sensation-packed descriptions of how, after parking their three cars on the Empire Road exit, they ask Mandisa what she thought she was doing. A screaming match between the two women ensues; it gets physical, with Kelly accusing Mandisa of wanting to kill her through her reckless driving. Kelly is arrested and carted off to Hillbrow police holding cells.*

As hard as I try, I'm never able to totally tune out of Kelly's dramatic life unfolding; especially when I see photos of her, smiling serenely and heavily pregnant. And then there are the ones of her holding Senzo's beautiful baby girl, stately and queenly content. I have never seen Kelly look happier. I read how Senzo tries to negotiate with his traditional Zulu family to take Kelly as his second wife. Negotiations fail. Senzo makes his choice. He embraces Kelly both privately and publicly into his life. Throughout it all, the insults in the press and on social media never abate.

I look for Kelly as I enter the front room steeped in sadness. Her mother, Ntombi, is holding their seven-month-old daughter. She is a little replica of her father. Her sister, Zandi, walks around dazed, not quite sure where she is going, what she is doing. I hug the two women. Whisper my condolences. I hold little Thingo. She is the only one smiling in the room.

"Where is she?" I finally ask.

"In the room, packing his clothes."

After shock, Death comes with such practicality.

She finally emerges, tiny and torn apart by tears. Her eyes break as she moves to me. We hold onto each other, weeping for what feels like a thousand years. I cannot speak. No words.

Later, squeezing together on a black beanbag, she will tell me what happened that night. The fear, the terror, the chaos. The gun cracking, tearing into her beloved's heart. How they raced him to the hospital through the darkness, across unforgiving potholes.

"I tried everything to save his life." Her tears spill.

By the time they got there he was barely breathing.

"He died in my arms, Melinda. I felt his body go cold. We were so happy. Everything had been moved out the way for us to love each other. Why ... why?"

I have no answer.

Later I will make her smile a little when I hold her and whisper: "Besides me, you are the bravest girl I have ever known. One day, I promise, you will wake up and it will be a little better."

As I embrace her little, grief-wracked body, I promise: I will throw fire at the haters.

She once told me, "The talent God gave me is bigger than the scandals, the drugs and mistakes I made with men."

I loved her for that. I could relate; scandalous mistakes were part of my life's CV.

"I am strangely peaceful," she says as I leave. "He is here. He will always be here."

Her love for Senzo is no mistake.

I stare at the notification for the disciplinary hearing. How can this be? This was a piece I wrote from the purest depths of my soul, for a sister publication, a newspaper within the group. I cannot see any conflict of interest, but now it appears that I am to be punished for it.

Authority. The stick. The threatening tone. It pushes all the buttons of my deepest fear and anger. I am thrown back in time to high school. Standing in front of the headmaster. I have been hauled before him after having sworn at the English teacher for failing me on my pre-final English essay because I wrote a poem instead of a long-form essay. I have always scored the highest marks for my creative work in English. Failing sends me careering over the edge.

My entire world falls apart as he barks away, telling me how much I have disappointed him and the staff, demanding that I give him back my prefect badge.

Now nearly three decades later, all the nausea that comes with fear and failure floods back. My eyes try to focus on the mail on my screen. I am asked to furnish all the details that led to me writing the Kelly story. Like a criminal, who is required to trace the lead-up to the night of a crime. The hair on my neck rises. I feel like I am being set up, trapped. But I know I have done nothing wrong.

If it comes down to it, I will not be ashamed to say to people: I got fired for writing a story on Kelly Khumalo, telling a story of a girl steeped in grief, who was treated like a woman waiting to be stoned at dawn.

My fingers tap furiously, quick as a sous chef's chopping knife, as I hammer out "my reasons" – I have no need to lie or fabricate facts. The email flies out my outbox. My heart is beating triple time. I can hardly breathe. I gather my things and leave the now-empty Friday, morgue-like office.

As I make my way down the long, empty passage, I feel a snake flick breath on my neck – the hooded Grim Reaper is nearing.

"They are trying to fire you," my insides tell me. It's too much of a coincidence – the timing – just a few days before the terms of my Ferrari disciplinary fall away. In fact, the date set for the new hearing is 1 December. The Ferrari disciplinary ends 2 December.

The lift creaks down to the ground floor. I sense the countdown to my exit has begun.

Over the weekend I start packing up my desk in my head. Making contingency plans. Spending over 10 years in one job requires a fair amount of mind shifting. My mental calculations tell me I have enough money stashed in my publishing house account and savings to be financially fearless for a little while. I will forsake medical aid. I will reinvest my retirement fund. So what if I lose the bags of freebie beauty products that already spill off my shelves and into every corner of my house? So what if I forsake the discounted deal on DStv? I will have to get used to doing without the comfort of a regular monthly salary but, quite frankly, it's high time I get brave and move on. Everyone has a date with The Machine.

Then I weigh up the idea of resigning.

I don't like the idea of it. I don't need to save face; I have done nothing wrong.

I have written from a place of love, honour and respect. And I am sure that I have made profit for the company as a whole.

Next week I will call my lawyer, but it will be more for reassurance than for advice. It is clear to me what the truth is. I find a strange sense of peace: I am done.

But for now I have other distractions. At the beginning of the week, I am off to Cape Town, for an end-of-year function with Land Rover Jaguar SA to celebrate their Good To Be Bad James Bond campaign and drive a range of gorgeous Jaguars. I will think about the hearing when I return. It's weird how cars keep taking me off to life-changing spaces.

CHAPTER 29

Tinderella and the Definition of Prosopagnosia

The gorgeous, cloudless Cape Town Tuesday is spent speeding around the peninsula in the F-Type Jag coupé and cabriolet. By nightfall we go off to our rooms to dress up for a murder mystery game, Cluedo style, to be played over a swanky dinner at the Hout Bay Manor where we are booked in for the night. We've been thoroughly briefed on our characters via email the week before, so we've all come pretty well prepared and dressed to the nines.

I am playing Lara Aziz, an assassin-type man-killer. I have a black, velvet, floor-length dress with thigh-high slits, an Uma Thurman *Pulp Fiction*-style shiny black wig, suspender tights and red lipstick. I feel pretty killer. But as the evening progresses and the rounds of shooters get more wild – and I'm not drinking – I decide to retire at about 11 pm. I always try to slip away unnoticed, a little embarrassed by my need to separate myself due to my sobriety.

Wig off and make-upless, I sit cross-legged on my hotel bed, and pick up my iPad. Time to post the pics of the night. Then something draws me to the little orange-flame Tinder icon. I haven't checked in for a while.

Logic tells me that, because Tinder is GPS-sensitive, and so location based, it seems stupid to log onto the dating app while I am in a different city, so far from home. I have set my search radius for 50 kilometres. But, what the heck, I'm far too hyped, far too sober to sleep. Besides, there's no harm in seeing if there's any truth to the perception that there are no hot single men in Cape Town.

Almost immediately the myth is dispelled. The first two guys look pretty cute. Quick swipes to the right, even though I know there really is no point – it's not like I will ever meet any of them. My plane leaves at 10 am, less than 12 hours from now. But this is fun.

Then the next pic comes up. I stop. Time freezes. Damn, damn, double damn – I feel like I am being pulled deep into the third eye of the very attractive profile photograph.

I scour his face, his eyes, looking for a clue … Who is this guy? I feel like I know him, I know him, I know him. Who, who, who? My brain tries to recall. I read his description. He sounds wonderfully witty and intelligent, but what really gets to me is a pic he has posted of a dusty skeleton, with the line: *Looking for the perfect woman.*

I swipe right.

Oh boy, how right he looks.

Almost simultaneously, my Tinder alert bell rings: *You have a match.* It sounds like the jackpot bells in a casino. Coins raining from the lucky-strike heavens. Angels singing on high. Dolphins leaping across a star-spattered sky. Bach violins swelling in crescendo.

You have a match.

I stare hard at the type that seems frozen on the screen. For a second it almost flickers neon silver.

I search the face of my match. Scour him for a clue, a sign, try to understand this overwhelming feeling of right.

What the hell, I am done with waiting. I take a deep breath, step toward the edge of the cliff and jump into the abyss of not knowing. I type: *I am sure I know you ... and this isn't actually Tinder small talk. I promise. Even though it sounds like it could be.*

I babble. I wait, not daring to breathe. Then: *Pleased to meet you again, Melinda. This life? Parallel universe? Previous incarnation?*

The relief rushes in. I breathe again. Smiling deep from within.

Me: *Maybe somewhere in the matrix. You look like someone I have met. It's very weird.*

Then he throws in the word that seals the deal: *Prosopagnosia.*

Not only is he quick, but he's funny too – and he uses words I have to Google! A word I don't know, from some guy on a social network! This makes such a change from the usual, unimaginative Tinder fare: *Hi* or *Hello* or *How are you?* Or my worst: *Hie.*

I type the word into the search engine: *Def: Prosopagnosia.* The response is *Face blindness. An inability to recognise faces.*

Well, fuck me slowly.

I am quietly blown away.

I take a breath, inhale. Almost immediately I am hurtling down the rabbit hole. I really want to find out more about this guy, so I keep talking.

I tell him I am on a car launch – it's actually part of my description, my online identity, where I mention that I can "torque Newton Metres". I have chosen this info specifically to set me apart from the Barbie doll brigade who list "cuddly toys" and "sunsets" as their interests. I name-drop Jaguar. I brag a little. I say I'm from Joburg and that I probably shouldn't have logged on since he's never going to have the sweet fortune of meeting me. Perhaps the time of night and knowing how much distance we will soon have between us gives me courage. I flirt a little. I flirt a lot.

I'm not sure why I am trawling Tinder at midnight in CT, I tell him. I turn the flirt button up a little further. *I must say the guys actually look better here than in Joburg.*

Then I decide to pull my killer line. In my short time on Tinder I have decided that this one separates the stupid from the intelligent ... the slightly off-beat ones, the crazy ones from the obtuse and mundane.

So, what's the worst thing you have ever done to a person ... living or dead?

I am surprised by his answer. I expect something clever but superficial. In the midst of all the witty banter, it suddenly goes serious.

Not holding on long enough to love.

The words hang in the air.

I am suddenly thrown by this intimacy.

And so I career into cars – meaningless banter on the F-type, the E-type. He asks me what else I do. I pull myself together and try to get a bit more real. I can sense he, this Tinder Dude, is all ears.

Me: *Besides being a Jag slag, a general car ho? I am a writer. A real writer. I write books.*

Tinder Dude: *What kind of books? What do you write about?*

Me: *Myself mainly. Drugs. Internal landscapes. Holes in the soul. Looking for more. More. More.*

Tinder Dude: *I know you. Oh yes, I fuqn do.*

I type: *I have a large brain. I hope that doesn't intimidate you* ☺

Tinder Dude: *It can never be large enough.*

His answer is instant. He confesses that he is a sapiosexual.

Ooh, a brain sex man – I am falling deeper by the minute.

Me: *A mind fucker.* ☺ *I like that.* ☺

Then it's star sign and career time.

Tinder Dude: *Virgo, Scorpio rising, psychiatrist.*

Me: *Leo. Cusp Virgo. Writer. Publisher.* Then, *Psychiatrist, yum. Free scripts ... free counsel.*

I half joke.

We both post emoticon yawns. Simultaneously. It's well past midnight. Fucking hell, we've been "talking" for almost two hours. Sleep time.

As I fall asleep, I think of him, 43 kilometres away. So near and yet so far. His is the first face I think of as I wake. I go back to our Tinder convo, almost wondering if I dreamt it. I reread it and smile.

When I land back in Joburg he has messaged me, with a sad face: *I see you are 1465 kilometres away* ☹

Over the following two days Tinder Dude and I message each other all day and late into the night. By Day 3 we leave Tinder, swap numbers and switch to WhatsApp.

By Friday, four days into our passion, the love drug effects have become almost unbearable. I wake up pre-dawn and know I need to see him. It's as though every minute apart is driving us insane. I know he feels it too. We are not even trying to play cool. We are both intrigued and amazed by our connection. When I manage to touch base with him mid-morning, between patients, and tell him about my idea to book a ticket to Cape Town to explore our connection, he responds as excited as I am. The decision is made.

Within minutes, the booking confirmation flies into my inbox. The phone alerts with an SMS. I take a screen grab and send it to him. He sends a stream of excited emoticons. It feels like I have just received my Master's degree in the post. The date to meet is set in stone. Now we just have to wait out the countdown. Seven more sleeps.

CHAPTER 30

It's a Match

The downer you experience from a high-dose dopamine love fest is a lot like coming down from a drug binge. In fact, there are many who believe experiencing love, coupled with a good spurt of lust, is as close as we may get to Nirvana on Earth – and even a bit like taking a shot of heroin.

Dopamine has all sorts of great feel-good effects: elation, high attention span and an increased ability to venture out and take risks, which of course is something I have never been short of. It's also a very seductive neurotransmitter for those of us prone to addictive behaviour and thinking, because it can so easily change a thought or a feeling into a habit.

There are even those who believe that the hunt for the dopamine high might actually be at the very core of, if not the sole "reason" or driver for addiction. And that elated feeling can feel very real and often very permanent. Dopamine, once released, can take days, even weeks to wear off before the body and mind get "sober" again.

On the flip side is prolactin, a hormone released straight after dopamine wears off, often bringing on a total downer, coupled with feelings of depression and depletion. Which explains the rather disturbing highs and lows we feel when we are in love.

And that's probably why ancient Taoists believed that nonorgasmic sex for men was the only way to go so as not to have to endure the heroin-like highs of dopamine and then the inevitable post-coke-like lows of prolactin. They also suggested that, in order to keep love flames burning in long-term relationships, distance and tension should be maintained to keep those loved-up dopamine levels high.

By the time Friday approaches, the day I am to fly to Cape Town, my excitement levels have all but shot through the roof. I am on a total high. But I seem to be the only one who is not a bundle of nerves; in the days leading up to The Big Date, my colleagues and friends have all voiced their grave concerns at my seemingly reckless plans. In fact, there are a few who think I am certifiably insane.

"What if he's a serial killer?"

"He could be Jeffrey Dahmer ..."

"Hannibal Lecter in *Silence of the Lambs* – psycho style."

I simply grin and brush their worried bleating away.

I am not in the least bit suspicious that Tinder Dude is a crazy. I have this deep feeling, this knowing, that everything will be more than okay. I simply can't let fear, doubt or neurosis get in my way. But I do have moments when I am terrified of more practical things. Like what happens if he isn't at the airport? Or, even worse, what if, when we get close, he smells weird? The smell thing is big for both of us. He says so too – a number of times. *I really hope you smell right,* he says in one of the many WhatsApps we have sent. Oh my fuck, I hope he likes Issey Miyake. But I have a feeling he doesn't mean perfume, that he means something far more carnal.

There's even a word for it.

I decide to impress him by naming it. If he can flaunt "prosopagnosia", I sure as fuck can throw in "olfactophilia". But, being a psychiatrist, he probably doesn't have to Google its definition.

The official definition for "olfactophilia", or "osmolagnia", is sexual arousal by smells and odours emanating from the body, especially the "sexual areas". Sigmund Freud, the granddaddy of psychoanalysis, eventually coined the term "osphresiolagnia" when referring to pleasure caused by odours.

Smell is central, for sure. But I am more seduced by sound – in other words, what emanates from the vocal organ.

"I hope I like your voice," I tell him the night before I fly out. "Do you have a heavy German accent?"

Up until this point we have not had a live conversation – everything has been online.

"If you have a heavy accent, I'm not sure I can deal with it, Goebbels. Führerfab is not really my thing," I venture, half joking. The childhood sounds of *Sieg heil* from old World War II Führer footage, inspired by my German mother's open admiration for Adolf, never fade as fast as the credits at the end of a normal movie.

It's Thursday night, 9 pm, the eve of my departure and I'm zipping up my suitcase when the phone rings. I see the number on the screen. Oh my fuck, it's him.

I chuck the offending machine on the bed and run out the room. It continues to ring back at me, accusingly. Finally it stops. I creep back into the room, stare at the missed call.

Get a grip, I tell myself, picking it up.

I know I am going to have to call back.

One, two, fucking three.

He answers, and I hear his voice for the first time. He sounds like he just flew in from the Fatherland.

"You really do sound like a German."

"I'm sorry."

We burst out in hyper-panicked laughter. We're both a bit breathless, jumbled; we talk on top of each other. We don't manage to keep a conversation going for more than 45 seconds before the real gets too much, we blurt our hurried goodbyes and hurtle back into our Virtual World.

What happens if we freak out when we see each other? If we can't actually speak live? I type frantically.

I've already got your WiFi spot organised in the garden, he fires back at me.

I find him hilarious – that's probably the very best thing about him, his sense of my special brand of off-the-planet humour.

At 2:46 pm the next day, I mutter excuses and leave work early to rush through traffic to make the 5:30 pm flight to land in Cape Town just after 7:30 pm. Check-in and boarding are a blur. We send each other a stream of excited WhatsApps until the plane has soared a couple of thousand metres into the big blue, soon-to-be-darkening sky.

The moment I walk through the Domestic Arrivals swing doors I see him, his head down, fingers furiously typing; I am sure it's to me. We have been messaging ever since I landed.

Time stands still. It is like a century passes. I have this feeling, clearer than anything I have ever known, that I am running towards my fate.

I creep up noiselessly behind him, whisper "Hello" in his ear. He's on his feet. He takes my face in both hands and stares long and slow, searching every part, inside me, down into the deepest place behind my shining eyes.

Into my arms, sings Nick Cave. *Into my arms.*

Within a few seconds our embrace becomes a kiss, bustling travellers, intercom announcements fading into the background. We're time travelling, leaving this place, this time, this airport far behind. It's a true moment of two hearts meeting.

The second we open his front door we find ourselves like two teenagers kissing slow and deep on the couch. Within three minutes we head to the bedroom and spend almost every one of the next 72 hours in amazed new blissfulness. It feels, it tastes, it sounds, it looks but most of all, it smells like love.

"Tinder was right," we giggle. "It's a match!"

Our parting three days later, and all those that are to follow, will take on epic proportions, like that of a Greek tragedy, as well as serious swings between dopamine and prolactin.

CHAPTER 31

Leaving The Machine

After meeting Tinder Dude – who is almost immediately christened Love of My Life – everything begins to feel different. I am suddenly infected with an almost superhuman surge of clarity, energy and courage.

After years of servicing The Machine, giving it my intellectual property, pitching up daily, writing copy, reading copy, editing copy, submitting copy, in and out, in and out, month after month after year, scanning my card through the boom, through countless other electronic gatekeepers, to get to my cage behind the big glass doors I call my desk, I finally realise that I am a number and my time to be crunched is on the cards. The Grim Reaper's breath hisses stale against my neck.

After the first hearing, when The Crash is generously settled by the company, and I am not dismissed, I immediately feel indebted. And even though I would really like to leave, break free, burst out of the doors and never come back, I stay. I am overcome with guilt, for being such a bad girl and costing The Machine so much. But staying over the past year has been pretty painful. Back from

Cape Town, I now know I need to leave. I have a deep feeling that my fate lies elsewhere.

The second hearing, the one in which I am accused of causing a conflict of interest because I have written a story on Kelly for a newspaper and not for The Mag, is scheduled to take place the day after I return from my weekend of love.

I feel extraordinarily calm. It's probably all the dopamine still surging through my system. Armed with a quickly prepared defence that a friend on Facebook has kindly put together via email after seeing a post of mine, I dress up once again in my LA Law Kenzo outfit. I decide to leave my hair unruly. Fuck it, this time I feel less of a need to impress.

The next two hours are spent in the ground-floor boardroom, where the chairperson hears the case brought against me by the business manager on behalf of the company. I am shocked when I see the thick file of evidence against me. I have clearly underestimated the seriousness of this case. My two-page printout of defence looks pathetic in comparison. The charges are read against me. I am being accused of losing money for The Magazine.

After the company's case is laid out – with the new editor acting as their star witness, highlighting how I have harmed The Magazine – it's my turn to defend myself. I have no witnesses; it's just me.

I explain the circumstances that led to writing the story. I try to make it clear that the new editor had every opportunity to ask me to write the story for The Mag because on the day I had told her where I was going, yet she had never asked me to write anything. I make it clear that instead of losing money, I have in fact made money for the sister newspaper and the group as a whole.

The company rests their case and states that they are seeking dismissal.

I am astounded. Tears spring to my eyes, but at the same time I am irritated with myself. What kind of Lala Land have I been living in? Of course they want me fired!

The chairperson, who works in another division but appears to be neutral, announces that there will be a recess during which time he will look at all the evidence before he makes a ruling. After an hour's deliberation, we are called back. I am suddenly absolutely freaked out, crunched up in a ball of terror. What if I am fired? Over something like this? It feels absurd. My brilliant career as a journalist is about to come to a humiliating, crashing end. Not with a bang, but with a bloody whimper. Fuck, fuck, fuck.

He reads out his judgment. It's close against my neck, the Grim Reaper's blade ... I can feel it. He finally announces the verdict: *Final written warning*. I am not fired. It feels like I have won at Le Mans. For a second my dignity, my being right, is restored. But that feeling doesn't last long.

That's a Tuesday. By Friday each hour that I am in the office feels like I am sniffing in toxic fumes. It just feels wrong to be here. There is no way I can eke the rest of my days out in this office, this Chernobyl. I need to go. I am planning to leave for Cape Town in a few days, to spend 16 days over Christmas to reignite my connection with Tinder Dude, during which time I will meet his two children. I am encouraged just by thinking of him, and even though we have only spent three days together in real time, I am fired up with hope when I think of the possibility of a beautiful life that may lie ahead of us. My crane swoops in.

I type up my resignation. I send a copy to the editor and one to HR. It's amazing how quick and simple it really is. Making the right decision and letting go of that which is bad for me.

My colleagues cry when I tell them I am leaving, that my time has come. Maybe my leaving will give them the space to do the right thing in their lives too.

I can see now how terribly tiresome I must have become for The Machine and those who run it – all my chaos, my creative moodiness, my messy edges, my screams and demands for truth and revision. Big business hates a firestarter, a troublemaker, a rabble-rouser. Over the past year, I have been all of that.

The Machine is about to forget me. It operates on strict orders. Once my resignation is processed, it will delete me and remove all trace of my existence.

And I know that I will soon forget it too. The human mind

can be a tabula rasa. Despite having woken up for 10 years at basically the same time each day, making coffee the same way, getting dressed, programming the house alarm with the same digits, locking the door, opening the remote gate, driving out along the road, looking left, looking right and heading across the city, off into the soulless bowl of traffic on the highway, swiping my access card, greeting the security guards, driving through the booms, parking in a parking lot, pushing the button on the lift to go up to Floor 2, walking out the lift, passing the receptionist, swiping my card again, through the access doors, to walk down the long, grey, open-plan office, to my desk, to sit down on my swivel chair, to turn on my computer, to log on – despite doing all of that, close to 2 500 times, despite all this deeply engrained ritual and habit, it's amazing how quickly my mind and body will soon forget. And just as The Machine has neutralised me, I will wipe my institutionalised memory clean. I can learn from The Machine. Accept. Delete. Move on.

The following day I decide to take the plunge and book a three-hour session with a tattoo artist. It's time to take a fucking risk and live again. I've been wanting to be inked for years. Later that afternoon in a tattoo shop on Grant Avenue, I have some of my favourite poetry carved into my flesh: *What we call the beginning is often the end. The end is where we start from.* Thank you Thomas Stearns Eliot.

The Machine can be an absent father.

A tattoo can be a soothsayer.

CHAPTER 32

Road Trip, Heart Trip

At just before 4:30 am, four days after I resign, I click the boot shut of the Honda Ballade I have been given for the December holidays. Like most new cars made in the second decade of the twenty-first century, it has a button on the key ring that opens the boot. It also has a great touch screen that makes it super easy to connect to Bluetooth and check data such as average fuel consumption. Although it's hardly a Ferrari, I am grateful that I have a new car to take me on my long adventure.

I've decided to throw caution to the wind, pack my boot with suitcases of clothes and shoes and head off into the great beyond – 1 476 kilometres, in fact – and spend time with the doctor who has Tindered my heart. I have never done road trips that have clocked up more than 800 kilometres. But, I tell myself, a self-respecting motoring journo needs to have notched up at least one solo trip down to Cape Town to give one a bit of endurance cred.

I resigned on a Friday, and now, four days later and infused with energy and the hope of new love, I am setting sail for exciting destinations. Some 16 days, 16 long days, stretch ahead with Tinder Dude – who has rather quickly become My Man – some of which will be spent with his two kids, a 10-year-old son and 12-year-old daughter. I am curious to see how we all get on together. That, I suspect, is going to be the real test ... I know these things well: if the kids don't like me, we may as well end it before it gets too painful. If they do, then we'll be in business. It's as simple as that.

It's still dark as I head out onto the highway. The all-knowing, all-seeing Google Maps speaks the way. But by 6:30 am, the roads are packed with travellers, like darts shooting from every corner of the concrete jungle to the ocean – spreading south, north, west and east – cars stuffed so full of holiday fare it's impossible for the driver to see out the back. Travelling during the pre-Christmas-time rush I develop a tinge of revulsion for humankind. At service stations where I stop to refuel and do a few star jumps to awaken my tiring mind, I bump into howling, bad-mannered kids, slip-slopped belly-hanging-over-shorts fathers and weary wrinkle-lined mothers worn thin by 12 months of endless demands.

On this journey I have much to think about. I process my resignation from The Magazine and everything that's happened in the past year: The Crash, the break-up with Ex-Boyfriend, the clinic, the meeting of Clinic Boy, the smoking, Oppikoppi, the break-up with Clinic Boy, Bikram, the giving up of cigars, Tinder, the hearing at work and the meeting of My Man. As I clock up mileage and the fuel tank dips, my mind empties and becomes clearer. I am transfixed by the glaze of endless horizons that melt away into the haze of burning tar. A road trip really is food for the soul. I see clearly now how endings hold the promise of new beginnings.

By 4 pm I have reached Beaufort West, established back in 1818 and often referred to as the capital of the Karoo. I had booked online a few days earlier to stay overnight in a B&B here in order to break the trip, sleep the night and restore my energy. About 900 kilometres of the 1 496-kilometre trip is done.

I check in, unpack a few things, shower, jump on the bed and attempt to take a nap, but however hard I try, I simply can't relax, never mind sleep; my eyes and brain are wide awake. Chill the fuck out, I tell myself, but, like a child before a big event, I am simply far too excited to see My Man, who I have been texting at every opportunity.

But, fuck this. I know I have paid for the room and I really should just surrender and force myself to sleep, but I cannot. So, after an hour, I gather my things together, take the keys back to reception and make my way back onto the highway, which has turned late afternoon golden. There are far fewer cars on the road now. The endless scar of tar etched out in the Karoo emptiness once again wills me on.

Nick Cave has been my driving companion on the long journey down. As I listen to his songs, from "Come Sail Your Ships" to "Push the Sky Away", I can feel the chambers of my heart opening as wide as the sky, filling up with love, as I navigate the final 300 kilometres. Nick reminds me that entire worlds have been built out of sorrow, of longing, but that they're only little tears. Lay your head on my shoulder, he sings, as the world beyond goes to war. *Are you the one that I've been waiting for?*

I surprise My Man about 200 kilometres out of Cape Town and message him that I am on my way. When I get to his house at 9 pm, it feels as if the stars really do explode in the sky. Like the roads I have navigated, cut out by our ancestors, veins that stretch across the land's beautiful valleys and plains, the long journey has sewn our souls together. Our reunion is memorable.

CHAPTER 33

The Insanity of Long Distance for a Girl with Separation Anxiety

Leaving My Man after 16 days of soul, body and heart connection feels like every inch of my being is torn apart by internally stitched Velcro. We remain in a love bubble of denial until two days before I am due to leave. Then, like some vagrant vampire, the reality of my imminent departure swoops in and hangs from the ceiling like a dirge.

Having spent almost every minute of the long Christmas holiday together, we've melted effortlessly into each other's lives. He's off from work, so we get to spend endless days that become nights that become days in his huge square bed, getting up only to throw meals together or occasionally go out into a world of "Jingle Bells" to garner supplies. We spend hours watching movies, YouTube and every episode of Ali G ever made. We laugh and laugh and shag and kiss and laugh until the ceiling spins. Sometimes his kids are with us, two beautiful beings who take me right into their arms and hearts.

I usually hate this time of year, dread it as it draws nearer and nearer, but this December it just flows easily and when the dreaded "Deck the Halls with Boughs of Holly" day comes along, his 12-year-old daughter urges me to download carols. Boney M's "Mary's Boy Child" bounces off the walls as we, giggling in aprons, prepare a huge roast chicken and potatoes. One afternoon, when on a rare occasion we leave the house, we visit Butterfly World where we are followed at every turn by a pair of beautiful birds. I am sure that within one of these feather-breasted creatures is the soul of my mother, an avid bird lover when she was alive, who has swooped in to show her approval.

But all too quickly the day that has been earmarked for departure screeches in.

I set the alarm for 5 am. It's 2 January 2015. I make sure I've packed everything up the previous night so all I need to do is get up very quietly, so as not to wake him or the kids, wash my face, dress and get out of there. I decide to do a French goodbye; no long, drawn-out partings, no tearful promises or last words together.

But just as I am about to close the door behind me I rush back to the bedroom and whisper a tiny love parting into his beautiful ear that beckons me like a little shell from the pillow.

And then I'm gone. Ignition on. Reverse, turn left, turn left again and then onto the long scar of the N2 that aches before me. This time, unlike my journey to meet him, there is no thudding heartbeat, no anticipation for the long wound of a trip that lies ahead.

The tears come later. In streams. Somewhere around Laingsburg – quite fitting, actually, since it was here where the famous floods of 1981 occurred. I was 14 years old when the state propaganda machine, SABC TV news broadcast pictures of the small town that had been swept away within minutes by one of the strongest floods ever experienced in the Great Karoo. A simple cloudburst, first praised and welcomed by the farmers, became a massive six-metre wall of water that rushed down the Buffels River and destroyed everything in its path. People, animals and possessions were swept along and later dumped under metres of life-stealing, unforgiving silt.

It is en route through this town that my heart's water breaks and I sob for the next two hours right until I get to Beaufort West. As the kilometres clock up, the dip down into prolactin is intense. By the time I get back to Joburg, it is night and the sky is as dark as my heart. As the longing and sadness set in over the next few days, the question I am forced to ask myself is why have I keyed into someone who lives 1 456 un-fucking-ruly kilometres away? All the separation anxieties I've harboured since childhood begin to gnaw away at me. So I try to write about it – unpack and expand on and write about love. I watch myself, like a surgeon may examine the brain of an etherised patient, sitting in front of my iPad, fingers poised, waiting for the usual stream to burst out my brain. I wait for that gush of uncensored words building thoughts into ideas into whole chapters and yet … The brain dries up. Bang, shut. Like a stake in the eye of a *Walking Dead* zombie. Like the slam of a door blown shut by some ill Harmattan, sweeping east across West Africa in some freak storm, all the way to Iran.

Up until I met someone who truly inspired me, I had never really wondered about it. Why was it so hard to write about Love? I mean, for me it's always been pretty easy to write about other four-letter words. Hate. Lust. Fame. Shop. Pain. Fear. Fuck(ing). But not *Love*.

So why is it that I feel so awkward naming it, describing it, unpacking and undressing it?

I decide to go back to God Google, and type: *Why is it so hard to write about love?*

Nothing. The search engine does not return a single result. There are hundreds for *Why is it so hard to write?* There are literally thousands for *Why is Miley Cyrus so crazy now?* There are about 20 for *Why is Steve Hofmeyr gay?* and there are even a few for *Why is Zuma building a bunker?* and *Why is Zuma a slut?* – but nothing about the trials of writing about love.

* * *

198

We are now forced to take to the virtual highways and byways courtesy of the Internet to stay in contact. WhatsApp and Facebook Messenger become cruel substitutions for skin-on-skin, tongue-to-tongue love we have just shared. Skype becomes the closest thing to real-time communication. There are some nights we lie on our beds, eyes drenched in our screens, locked in virtual embrace as we Skype on and on for hours, losing ourselves in the one-dimensional patterns of our faces. I grow to love the pixelated shadows of his profile during storms and bad reception. It is only when it's time to say goodbye and close the app that the thud and the ache in the chest comes. The second after the little red Off icon is pressed, the aftermath of that elastic silence stretches across the world and bounces back to sting me in the face.

There is nothing as hollow as the end of a lover's Skype call.

Airports become morgues when departing from him; aeroplanes on runways are hearses. On trips to see him, they are chapels of joy. I become fascinated by aerodynamics and am constantly amazed that 400 tonnes of wire, passengers and metal can stay airborne and travel thousands of kilometres across the sky and not fall, and how far we've come since December 1903, when the Wright brothers flew the first plane, a flight that lasted just 12 seconds and covered less than 122 feet.

Trips to Cape Town are booked, wangled when they can for an event or a launch, even for the opening of an envelope. Air miles accumulate, collect up in the sky, 38 000 feet above sea level, then down, to land, Joburg–Cape Town–Joburg–Cape Town, up and down, up and down. I become one of the 56 million people on the planet who fly weekly.

We soon establish a pattern in which I travel down about every fortnight to spend on average six days together before I need to fly back to Joburg to see my sons and do my radio car show, *The Joy Ride* on Kaya FM, on a Thursday night.

The lead-up to meetings are filled with rising adrenalin, the dreaming for days before our reunion. Four sleeps. Three sleeps. Two sleeps. The passionate embraces after weeks of longing.

The intensified love-injected days together, when every moment is stretched out a little longer than mundane real time, are gravity-defying miracles. And then before we know it, the day of leaving arrives, like some insolent student too early for class.

Partings are top of our lists of The Things We Most Hate on Our Planet. The tearing away of body and soul can feel like a loss of life. Little deaths. No – huge, heartless, all-encompassing deaths. The depth of the dying depends on how many days we have intersected.

I always try to wake before the dark has lifted, him still deep in a slumber, and creep out of the still-curtained room that carries the smells of all our love and drag my clothes on in the lounge, my suitcase standing at the front door like a stern sentinel, all packed and ready the night before. Just before I leave, I usually run back and slip a silent kiss on his neck and a little lick in his ear and hurry away before he realises I am gone.

All we have to look forward to is the Resurrection, to the day when we shall see each other again. And then two or three days before we do, the elusive horizon suddenly appears faint but glisteningly real, and I know what a sailor must have once felt when he saw the promise of land after years at sea, back when men still thought you could fall off the edge of the world.

And so we go about it all again – our hellos and goodbyes.

To make me feel better I sometimes convince myself that this long-distance thing kind of suits me, that it's what I want, that the hypomanic girl in me – addicted to drama, to the ups and downs and rose-tinted specs – actually likes the way this is because it perfectly protects me from emotional intimacy, the very thing I longed so much for when I was with Ex-Boyfriend, but of what I'm probably most terrified.

But most times, when I am being honest with myself, each time I say goodbye to My Man, it feels like my insides become grated shreds of loss. And it is the connection of emotion that I long for most.

In one of our many Messenger exchanges, I tell him I am the strongest woman he will ever meet. *The strongest woman in the world*, I call myself. I also slip in that I'm the biggest baby, the deepest, blackest hole and most changeable female he will ever lay eyes on. I add that I give great head and I will make sure that, whatever happens between us, I will be unforgettable.

He appears to be intrigued. He is particularly keen on the "strongest woman" – yes, the "giving head" gets a smiley emoticon, but it's clear that it's the brave one he's really after.

As time slips by and forced separation becomes part of the deal, I realise how much strength is indeed needed for this long-distance adventure. If nothing else, it's a brutally accurate barometer of whether you are in or out, whether your heart is in it for the long haul or if this is just a little summer fling, a deviation or a seductive distraction. Because the little deaths that come with the pain of every parting are definitely non-negotiable and grow a little more severe with each goodbye.

The rose-tinted, loved-up specs have been perched on our noses for almost half a year, and our seamless compatibility astounds us.

And then we have our first real argument.

It seems to come out of nowhere – and to me it feels like the temple curtain of our love has torn in two. I want to panic, bolt, run away, grab the keys of the sexy wheels parked outside, turn on the ignition and hurtle away like a rocket, zero to 100 in four seconds. On a Mad-Maxed road trip. Escape from the Alcatraz of the heart. But somehow I don't. I stay.

After the emotional dust has settled, he urges me to embrace these times of conflict because it is inevitable that there will be more and, in the end, these are the things that really count when the dopamine fades, when reality sets in. The test of a good relationship is about how well you make up after a fight. I am forced to really look at myself in these achingly uncomfortable moments of conflict.

I am amazed at just how this big mouth, confident blabber is actually sometimes a terrified little mouse who abhors conflict and how, at the first opportunity, I run and hide. It feels like I have been fleeing forever, like one of Daenerys Targaryen's fire-breathing dragons, flexing my Pegasus wings, running off the edge of the cliff and leaving the conflict behind me. The threat of losing love, especially, makes me do it.

But the escape is all in my head, because more often than not my bolting is internal. I don't have to move an inch. I curl up inside like a foetus in the womb, my fingers in my ears to block out the noise, my heart racing against fear – fisting it deep within, killing my shame, my need, my fear so that no one will see or hear. And usually the one I hurt most, the one I strike out hardest against is myself. A fistful of cobra.

Unlike the conflict I experienced in previous relationships, now with My Man I somehow find a way to stay, and I mean really *stay* – to sit with it, engage and see the emotions through. It's like I have chewing gum on my seat; it's messy, it's sticky, it's not a pretty picture, but instead of bolting, I stay. Somehow he makes me. He swallows up my fears. We sweat it out.

And I begin to understand what emotional intimacy is all about.

But arguments are far and few between. There are many languid weekends when we lie on his triple king-size bed as day turns to night turns to day, staring into the velveteen of each other's eyes, our love growing in dolphin leaps and far away, thunderous waves celebrating with trumpet calls that rebound across the universe.

We begin to talk about what would happen if we actually gave it a go, and found a way to be together every day. We are wistful; it seems like an unreal dream on some distant shore. My house in Joburg begins to feel like a jail. It seems like the nights we spend on Skype are becoming impossibly tormenting.

When I am not flying to and fro, when I feel all alone and miss My Man too much, 40-degree Bikram studios become my distraction, my father, mother, therapist, surrogate lover. I begin to look forward to the 90-minute classes, ache for them, long for them, like a cigarette, like a daily ritual.

They say that yoga heals the soul. I know that it stretches my body, and sometimes the salty sweat from my limbs makes its way to my heart and then seems to ease my fears.

Yoga also stops me thinking. It's an antidote for the Obsessive Compulsive Disorder and Toxic Brain Syndrome I have decided to diagnose myself with when my mind becomes too strong to handle. After about four months back in the Bikram rooms, I find out one day that it's not the spine-twisting, back-bending, muscle-wrenching postures that most challenge me, but *savasana* – the Dead Body Pose, the posture of relaxation.

In Bikram yoga, it's done the first time halfway through the 26 postures after the standing series, for two whole minutes – which doesn't seem so long, but for me it is sometimes an eternity. *Savasana* was specially designed to happen at this juncture, about an hour into the practice, to allow the blood to flow throughout the body, creating a rush of internal cleansing after the pretty hardcore postures preceding it. It's believed that this is when the real magic of yoga happens, when authentic physical and subsequent mental healing can take place.

And this, I find, is by far the hardest thing to which to surrender. To rest. To be still. To be quiet within myself. To stay. I have never been good at sitting in silence, doing the whole "Ohm, ohm … I am at one with the universe" thing. In active addiction, I chose to use drugs to find Nirvana and, in recovery, over the years, I have drowned myself in work to get into a coma.

But early one morning something happens at the end of the class. Flat on my back, mat and towel drenched in salty sweat that has made its way everywhere, even streaming into my eyeballs, I stop. Everything. And for the longest moment all goes quiet.

And, in that eternal nothing, the huge empty universe wraps around me. And then an echo of an echo. It is the same non-sound that swirled me in white light as the Ferrari, my sukkot, spun and spun and spun before it stopped and I was dragged, like a baby bird falling, from the precipice of death.

I know that it is the Divine that has come to breathe with me. And show Itself. And for a moment the hole, the wound, the emptiness becomes full.

And all is exactly the way it should be.

Learning to stay in *savasana* begins to teach me that perhaps I am getting ready to stay with love, to risk my heart again. To stop the to and fro, up and down of hello and goodbye, death and resurrection. A few days later, I decide to contact an estate agent to discuss putting my house in Joburg up for sale.

CHAPTER 34

The Owl House

My Man and I take a road trip through the Karoo and decide
to make a detour past the village of Nieu-Bethesda in search of
the Owl House. Ever since I was in my teens, when I first heard
about Helen Martins – the woman who owned the house – I've
wanted to see her art for myself, her huge collection of concrete-
and-glass statues.

But little prepares me for the overwhelming sense of pain and
recognition as we walk through the yard where over 300 artworks,
including owls and Christian and Eastern figurines, fight for every
available space in the small village garden. I immediately sense the
mania attached to her output. At one point it is almost too hard to
take it all in. I sit on a little ledge among the owls and the angels,
and close my eyes to escape the intensity. But, unable to block it
all out, instead I get a rush of images of Helen working in a frenzy,
mixing clay, shaping figures, creating, creating, fighting her death
urge. It is like I am on some acid trip, like everything is moving in
to throttle me. I suddenly feel very tired. I long to lie on a soft bed
and blot out the images of her deep and dark mind space.

But it doesn't let up. I am overwhelmed by an intense connection with Helen, getting up each day to create each of the
concrete effigies, many of whose arms and hands desperately reach
toward some sun or imaginary light. I am suddenly reeling from

recognition of a similar impulse in me. That bone-deep need to push the pressing-down sky away each day.

I am only half aware of tears running down my cheeks when I feel my love touching me gently on the shoulder. I know he can see right into me. As I open my eyes and come back into the garden I am struck by the stark blue sky, the blinding Karoo sun.

We move inside, look at the little bed, the mirror, the faded copy of the *Mona Lisa*, the lonely coffee cups. I sense how, as her sight and health began to fail her, at the age of 75, Helen got up one day, no longer able to walk into the light, no longer able to feel the sun on her skin. One day the fight simply got too much. That day she swallowed a mixture of caustic soda and crushed glass. She took her own life. Images of dark times in my past flash through my mind, times when I had to drag myself up and fight for the light, sometimes on an hourly basis. The killing of the death urge, the eating up of the death hunger.

I have known these moments well. I know that day could have happened to me; I could so easily have woken up and decided to end it all. I know it could happen to any one of us who struggles to make sense of this world, who feels that pull towards the darkness. Standing, staring at my reflection in her glass, I vow to myself to keep seeking clarity, to keep walking towards the light.

If Martins had been examined by shrinks today, I am sure she would have more than likely been diagnosed with something similar to what I've been labelled: Bipolar 2, mania. Perhaps that's why I feel such deep recognition. She would have been stamped with some disorder that would have seen her medicated and dulled, dispirited and laid to rest in the House of Numb. Doctors would have taken that free and beautifully crazy spirit of hers and evened and ironed it out, creating some castrated version of the self. She would not have woken each day to the urge to fight against the dark and impending sky. She would not have made this garden of concrete and house of glass.

When we get home, My Man guides me through the final stages of stopping my psych meds all together. I start to feel the deep urge to write again.

CHAPTER 35

You Can Only Keep What You Have By Giving It Away

*"Treat people as if they are what they ought to be,
and you help them to become what they can be."*
– VIKTOR FRANKL, QUOTING JOHANN WOLFGANG
VON GOETHE

A few weeks after our visit to the Owl House, I find myself back in Joburg, that powerless, long-distance pain of being away from My Man gnawing at me. I have just had my first show day, and there have been no offers from prospective buyers of the house. I feel in limbo.

To distract myself, I have decided to sign up for a Master's in Recovery Coaching being facilitated by David Collins, a successful recovery and life coach who was also my first sponsor in NA. I often wonder what would have happened in my life if I hadn't met Dave, who in my early recovery dragged me through many brutal hours, days when I would much rather have given up on life than live through it. If there is such a thing as a person "saving" another then he was certainly my addiction Superman.

As I walk into the first session, slap bang into a circle of strangers, I am not entirely sure why I am really doing this. For the past few years I have balked at even the slightest idea of officially working in the world of recovery. Besides, I have convinced myself that I have been doing enough in terms of the all-important Step 12 of the NA programme, which advises to "spread the message to the addict who still suffers". I have told myself over and over that writing my two addiction-related books, *Smacked* and *Hooked*, has been more than adequate in terms of paying it forward. The truth, however, is that I have lost sight of the bigger picture, too busy being busy in the real world to put myself out and really reach out to the addicts around me.

I'm unenthused and resistant as I take my place among the course students. My feelers are on what I like to call "high suspicion for bullshit" alert; in reality, that usually means that I am feeling a lack of love, terrified and defensive. I look around the room of strangers and make quick judgements of all the participants. The blonde one's too uptight, the other's too jolly-hockey-sticks, the brunette's really depressed and messed up ... But, of course, I soon discover that these superficial judgement calls are simply the ones that shield me from my real ones: that I'm actually really uncomfortable with being here in all my stark and vulnerable sobriety, that meeting people for the first time always freaks me out, sends me into a panic, and that, in order to compensate, I usually resort to my super-confident, loud-mouth personae. No wonder, pre-recovery, I loved downing a couple of tequilas, snorting a few lines, and smoking heaps of smack before strutting into a club or a party.

Once the group settles down, we form a container and check in by introducing ourselves and naming our feelings. It soon dawns on me that I'm part of an amazing group of powerful women: a social worker, a few counsellors, a metal worker, a filmmaker, an events planner and a few community activists. As group members share personal details about themselves I watch from above and wonder what I want these people to know about me, how I want them to see my person. I try to resist my usual go-to space, be the one who wants to talk about all my outside achievements, about all that I do, and the ways I have succeeded in the world.

The next two days see something quite unprecedented happen to me. I drop the need to look good, successful and together, and I leap into the unexplored. I am not sure if I have ventured there in over 15 years. Not since I was down on my knees in the black hole, the space between life and death, when I found myself lost and dispossessed on the homeless farm I write about in *Smacked*. And how, in that desperate and terrified space, I found the faith to leap over the cliff into the Great Unknown and fall deep into the ravine where vultures feast on the bones of the faithless and eagles dip and soar with the souls that are saved. It was there, in that magic place between life and death, that I was granted a wing and a prayer to rise up on, where I learnt about faith, to ask for help and where I learnt how to fly.

But I soon found out that the act of flying doesn't in itself guarantee a cure for the hole in the soul. And despite, over the last decade and a half, spending thousands and thousands of rand on therapy, to find the source of that first wound that influenced everything, in a desperate attempt to uncover the button to reset me, I have not had much success.

But on the final day of our first module, as we are checking out of our container – our close-knit group – out of nowhere a messenger from the gods, a crane, flies in to lift me and take me to the tree top of my soul. It happens almost imperceptibly, a pinprick that hits me right in my heart's centre, the place that ached so much in my *ustrasana*, the Camel Pose in the Bikram class. For a moment I can hardly breathe; it feels like it will consume me. Tears streaming, after what feels like a lifetime of silence, I find it in me to touch the point of my pain that is so deep, so old within me. In that moment I realise that I've never allowed myself to really cry or feel sad, to grieve the death of my father. I have blocked it out for years. Covering it over with layers and layers of denial and avoidance.

This truth inside opens up my sky, my tears spill and I cry. And cry. Now a crane and the container hold me and my pain moves out of me like a surly snake that's been holding me in bondage for what feels like a million years. If this is all I have come for, I have come for enough.

I check out the container: "I feel real."

CHAPTER 36

How Trashing
a Ferrari Saved
My Life

As I near the final straits of my book, I travel to the ocean, to the same beautiful beach house where I sought refuge in order to finish my other two books, *Smacked* and *Hooked*, part of this, my memoir trilogy. I am an author in search of an ending.

Here on the deck I roll out my yoga mat each morning to the distant sound of sea gulls that call to me across the water, and somewhere in the big house is the laughter of my two beautiful teenage sons – my true northern stars. I stand on one leg and I do my Bikram Tree Pose. And breathe.

There is something so simple, so predictable about the tides, the silvery waves rolling in and out, that they give me a sense of perspective and remind me how very small I really am. I think about a time long ago when I had nothing but a broken soul; homeless, derelict, lost, a time when I had truly abandoned myself and how so much has changed for me over the last 16 years, since I became clean and sober.

Then my mind swoops back to two years ago, and how it almost went so terribly wrong, when six lives came within nanoseconds of a head-on collision with Death. How my entire world, the one I had worked so hard to build up, felt like it was imploding, crashing into chaos, as I tried to slam on the brakes of the multimillion-rand Ferrari, which spun out of control, like a demented whirling dervish. And gratitude for life floods in.

My mind shifts into reverse, back to the year that followed The Crash and the challenges that felt like they would kill me: massive legal bills, the threat of being fired hanging over my head, total mental meltdown, a clinical diagnosis, post-traumatic stress, a R200-a-day cigar habit, a torn and shattered heart – at the time, it all seemed too much to bear and there were many days that I ached for a drink, a hit, a puff of Morpheus oblivion.

But somehow I didn't.

Now I think of myself before The Crash and the collision course I was riding: arrogant, seduced by my own omnipotence and silly outward successes, adding my weight and ignorance to the planet, heaving under an ever-growing heap of rubbish. Now seeing my own carelessness in a world where 222 million tonnes of food are wasted a year in the West, almost the entire net food production of sub-Saharan Africa.

I see how I became part of the consumerist cancer, kitted out in my clever clogs, my stupid preoccupation with Kenzo and Blahnik and Timberland; boxes and boxes of cosmetics – anti-ageing, anti-wrinkle landfills of time-defying jars, empty illusions conjured up by a multibillion-dollar beauty industry. Ludicrous labels making absurd promises to wall the inevitable dam of time that comes crashing down on all of us, regardless of how many millions you have in the bank, how many kilos of whale sperm serum we slap on our faces, or how many monkeys need to be tortured in the process.

Images of my creative and spiritual bankruptcy after years of toil in The Machine flood in – churning out meaningless drivel about sex and relationships, soulless rubbish on how to turn him on, how to tell if he's a keeper, 10 ways to know that he's cheating – when I had lost all ability and instinct to sense it when it was happening in my own life, under my very own nose. Believing in nothing more than in the power of Me. Pride cometh before a fall, the cliché warns. And it's right. It does.

I realise how my arrogance made me forget who I was and where I came from. With all my outward successes, I had forgotten that the rooms – the NA fellowship meetings – had once been my circle of refuge, the place that had saved me and guided me into a new way of life. I forgot about the philosophy of paying it forward. Slowly, I had withdrawn from my fellows, concentrating on our differences rather than our similarities, at times even reviled by the broken addict that was, more than ever, alive and kicking in me.

The sea shows me how addicted I had become to the process of trying to recover. All the missions I have been on to score a better life after the drugs stopped: the books I have read, the meetings I have attended, the groups I have joined, the yoga poses I have bent in, the men I have looked to and replaced God with, the reams and reams of white paper I have written on, searching for meaning, etched in black-blood hieroglyphics.

I see now how The Crash stripped the scales from my eyes. And how, by accepting what had happened – being a little Buddhist and a little Nietzchien about it, letting go of the bad, and "loving my fate" – what a massive learning curve it has become and continues to be for me.

I see now how, if there was no Crash, I wouldn't have gone to the clinic, met Clinic Boy, broken up, signed up on Tinder and met My Man and how tomorrow even more connections will be revealed. I see how everything is connected and how it must all be. *Es muss sein.*

After a week at the ocean, I drive down the street towards my house in Joburg, my almost finished book safe on my iPad. My home has had its third show day and as yet no offers. I am panicking. Why hasn't it sold yet? Perhaps I need to drop my price, get rid of it, make a plan. I am tired of the long-distance stresses, of the not-knowingness. I want to be with My Man. Now.

As I pull up after 5 pm, I notice that the agent is still on the property. Damn. I really need to take a bath, unpack.

Then I hear my name and I realise that the smiling woman walking excitedly down my drive towards me is one of my Bikram yoga teachers. In the next few minutes I hear how she and her fiancé are in love with my house, how she wants to turn my cottage into a yoga studio. Twenty minutes later we sign an offer. Three weeks later I begin packing up to move to Cape Town, to start a new life in a new city, next to My Man, side by side. Perhaps happy endings do happen after all. ☺

But punching through the swelling pink-tinted final credits I so long for, I sense on the other side that there is a chasm of terror that grips me – the challenges and changes that a relationship of substance and intimacy will inevitably bring, when days are bleak and tempers are frayed, when that rosy cloud eventually turns grey, and conflicts inevitably arise. How will I cope then?

Am I strong enough to be real and not switch and change and avoid? Will I be able to rise above uncomfortable feelings, bruised emotions, fear and distrust and *stay*?

I am not sure how I will do it, but I do know that I want to see what happens when I sit with the small and often sad me, when I no longer fill the silence with a diversion or distraction, when I force myself to stay in *sivasana*. And what will happen if I believe in love?

* * *

A few weeks before I move, I am approached to share my story with a group of homeless people in Cape Town who gather each day at a soup kitchen on the outskirts of the CBD. As I walk in, I am all too aware of how this tough-as-concrete audience will perceive me: rich, stuck-up bitch driving a swanky car, carrying an expensive handbag stuffed with wads of cash ... What could she possibly have to say? How could she know how it feels to walk in broken, mouldy shoes, and sleep under folded cardboard boxes, under the bridge downtown, on freezing stormy nights?

I breathe in deep and tell them I know exactly what they are thinking and how they perceive me. I sense they are far from buying it, but as I begin to share my tale of how a nice successful middle-class girl who was a prefect and top achiever hit skid row on a hellish bender in search of a hit and a high, I feel them start to listen. By the time I get to the part of my tale that sees me hacking, penniless and homeless, I have their buy-in. We are one.

And so when I begin to tell them how my healing started the day that I woke up on the homeless farm, and realised that I could no longer blame anyone else for my sad, sorry, dispossessed life – that it was I, me, who needed to stand up and take responsibility for the mess I was in – I sense light bulbs turn on in the room. There are truly those who understand what I mean.

Hamlet says, "Nothing either good or bad, but thinking makes it so …" Perhaps this is the greatest lesson I learned when I got clean, and remember each and every day 16 years later. What we think, we manifest. What we think we are, we are.

Whether I'm in a 5:30 am sweaty Bikram studio, out on the road in a new ride, laughing with my boys, struggling to make sense of pain, injustice and poverty, doing a talk about recovery to the broken or waking up next to My Man, I know that we can choose our own routes.

"Our brains are like machines. Like big computers," I tell the hollow-eyed men. "Whatever we feed them, that's what we become. Our thoughts are everything. So if you walk around each day and say, 'I am a loser, I am a failure, I am homeless, my life is fucked up', so shall it be."

The room is clear and silent. My heart space grows.

"But within us we each have the power to change this often terrible script that resembles our life. To say no, that this isn't how it has to be. Today, as I stand here in front of you, I swear that I have been where you are, and if I – this fucked-up, hopeless addict – can change, so can you."

At the end of my talk a number of the men come to me and tell me their stories. As I leave, there is a brightness in the room. I sense the sweet smell of possibility, of change.

Ten days later I offer to do a few coaching sessions with two members of the homeless group. I hear stories of brutal hardship. I can relate to some of their pain. At the end of our second session, I give them each a little black journal and a pen, small enough to fit into their pockets.

"When you are all alone and you are feeling like the world has forgotten you, write. Write your worst thoughts down, things you have never told anyone. Things you don't even know about yourself. Write what you hope for, what you dream. Recording my thoughts in a little book is what saved my life long ago; it might help in saving yours. You are in a good space to change. You have nothing more to lose."

They leave with their books. And wide smiles.

The circular shapes and patterns of life are not lost on me. How, once homeless, and now restored and alive, I return to a place to speak to those who have nothing, a place where I can now humbly go, to reach out to others and hold them within.

"What we call the beginning is often the end, the end is where we start from."